India and the Bomb

Notre Dame Studies on International Peace
Joan B. Kroc Institute for International Peace Studies
University of Notre Dame

With the end of the Cold War the promise and relevance of peace research have significantly increased. The issues now addressed include the nature of the world order, international institutions, the resolution of deadly conflicts, humanitarian security, and ethical issues raised by violence, environmental degradation, and poverty. Peace studies probe these problems and search for comprehensive solutions.

Notre Dame Studies on International Peace focuses on these vital issues. Scholarly perspectives are combined with sound policy recommendations and the setting of normative standards. The books published here emanate primarily from the research work of the Kroc Institute and its other activities, especially the annual Theodore M. Hesburgh, C.S.C., Lectures on Ethics and Public Policy.

Joan B. Kroc Institute for International Peace Studies was established at the University of Notre Dame in 1986. In addition to research projects, the Institute has an international graduate program and an undergraduate concentration in peace studies. It is a premier institute in its field in the United States. More information can be obtained from the Kroc Institute, P.O. Box 639, University of Notre Dame, Notre Dame, IN 46556, USA (phone 219-631-6970, fax 219-631-6973).

India and the Bomb
Public Opinion and Nuclear Options

EDITED BY
David Cortright
and Amitabh Mattoo

WITH A PREFACE BY
Raimo Väyrynen

University of Notre Dame Press
NOTRE DAME, INDIANA

Copyright © 1996
University of Notre Dame Press
Notre Dame, Indiana 46556
All Rights Reserved

Manufactured in the United States of America

Library of Congress Cataloging-in-Publication Data

India and the bomb: public opinion and nuclear options / edited by David Cortright and Amitabh Mattoo.
    p.   cm.
    "A publication of the Joan B. Kroc Institute for International Peace Studies"— ISBN 0-268-01176-1 (alk. paper)
    1. Nuclear weapons—India—Public Opinion. 2. Upper class—India—Attitudes. 3. Nuclear weapons—Government policy—India. 4. Public opinion—India. I. Cortright, David, 1946-.
II. Mattoo, Amitabh.
U264.5.I4I63   1996
355.02'17'0954—dc20   95-50914
                                                                                                 CIP

∞ *The paper used in this publication meets the minimum requirements of the American National Standard for Information Sciences—Permanence of Paper for Printed Library Materials, ANSI Z39.48-1984*

Contents

Preface vii
   Raimo Väyrynen

Acknowledgments ix
About the Contributors xi

Map of India xiii

Indian Nuclear Policy Options

  1 **Indian Public Opinion and Nuclear Weapons Policy** 3
     David Cortright and Amitabh Mattoo

  2 **Abstaining: The Nonnuclear Option** 23
     Kanti Bajpai

  3 **Status Quo: Maintaining Nuclear Ambiguity** 53
     Aabha Dixit

  4 **Freeze: Halting the Testing and Development of Nuclear Weapons** 69
     Sumit Ganguly

  5 **Going Nuclear: Establishing an Overt Nuclear Weapons Capability** 85
     Varun Sahni

Appendices

  A **An Analysis of the Kroc Institute Survey** 109
     Jackie G. Smith

  B **Complete Results and Tabular Data of the Kroc Institute Opinion Survey** 117

  C **MARG Survey Questions** 135

Bibliography 145
Index 155

Preface

Nuclear weapons and the doctrines of their employment are among the most significant public policy issues to be imagined. Yet they are surrounded by secrecy, and often the "nuclear estate" has deliberately spread false information either to mislead people or calm public fears. In the case of the U.S. nuclear arsenal the complex combination of deception, ambiguity, and strategic calculations is well told in a recent book by Jay Robert Lifton and Greg Mitchell, *Hiroshima in America: Fifty Years of Denial.*

Yet the average American probably knows more about nuclear policy than the average British, Chinese, French, or Russian citizen, in whose countries strict rules of secrecy have prevailed. Even in democracies it has been difficult to obtain reliable information on the size of nuclear arsenals, command-and-control procedures, and other key issues. In autocratic countries obtaining such information may be impossible and is often punishable by law. Nuclear weapons information is considered the exclusive property of the state and is not to be shared with ordinary citizens.

Secrecy and punishment have also prevailed in so-called threshold countries, such as Iraq, Israel, Pakistan, North Korea, and South Africa, which have been clandestinely developing "bombs in the basement." In this context India is an intriguing case. It distinguishes itself from other threshold countries by having time-honored democratic traditions, strong mass media, and active public opinion, all contributing to a rather high degree of openness in society.

Yet, most Indians feel that the established nuclear powers have appropriated an undue amount of political international influence through their nuclear weapons status. Many Indians favor the development of nuclear weapons as a means of gaining such influence for their country. The nuclear weapons option has also been defended by the argument that India's security is seriously threatened by Chinese and increasingly by Pakistani nuclear weapons. Thus both India's international standing and security are often thought to require nuclear weapons, or, at a minimum, a capacity to produce them when needed.

Against this backdrop the opinion survey conducted and interpreted by David Cortright, Amitabh Mattoo, and their collaborators provides an interesting glimpse into the thinking of Indian elites on nuclear weapons and prospects for their dismantling. It is the first comprehensive survey on the topic in India. As such, the survey increases the transparency of nuclear weapons policies and contributes to a democratic political debate.

Extensive reporting of the survey findings in the Indian press in 1995 has probably also expanded public knowledge of nuclear weapons issues and options in India. Public debate on nuclear weapons is particularly important now that the international political and military environment has undergone significant changes. Great powers are cutting back their nuclear arsenals, the Nuclear Nonproliferation Treaty (NPT) has been prolonged indefinitely, a comprehensive test ban is in sight, and discussions are underway for a ban on the production of fissile material. This progress in nuclear arms control may be creating a quandary for Indian public opinion. The two central determinants of Indian policy—support for global nuclear disarmament and the defense of India's political and military autonomy—are clashing. This means that the traditional policy of nuclear ambiguity, though still enjoying extensive support among Indian elites, is under increasing pressure. As a result, New Delhi may be forced to make more explicit choices regarding nuclear weapons, favoring rather than opposing them.

The survey commissioned by the Fourth Freedom Forum and the Joan B. Kroc Institute for International Peace Studies gives reasons for concern. The finding that one out of three elites favors an overt nuclear weapons capability suggests that nuclear weapons will become increasingly important to the future security of South Asia. It would be too easy, though, to criticize the Indian elites for having a penchant for weapons of mass destruction. The survey shows that the pressure to acquire nuclear weapons would considerably diminish in India if a time-bound global agreement to give up nuclear weapons could be reached and a regional arrangement to restrain nuclear weapons and build confidence could be established. Indians widely believe in general and complete nuclear disarmament.

This survey of Indian elites provides yet another argument for serious global and regional efforts to move to the postnuclear era. It shows clearly that a regional security arrangement would increase Indian willingness to accede to the NPT. It also indicates that a serious disarmament policy on the part of the major powers would have a positive effect in reducing the desire for nuclear weapons in South Asia.

Raimo Väyrynen
Joan B. Kroc Institute for International Peace Studies
University of Notre Dame

Acknowledgments

This book has benefited from the assistance and support of many friends and colleagues. First we wish to express our gratitude to those who provided the financial support and inspiration for undertaking this study of public opinion and nuclear options in India. We are most grateful to George Perkovich, director of the Secure Society program at the W. Alton Jones Foundation. Perkovich not only offered funding assistance but also helped to guide the project with his own expert understanding and analysis of South Asian nuclear policy. We are indebted to Tom Graham of the Rockefeller Foundation for supporting a program of visiting scholars to the Joan B. Kroc Institute for International Peace Studies at the University of Notre Dame and for sparking the ideas that led to this project. We owe our greatest debt to Howard Brembeck, founder and chairman of the Fourth Freedom Forum, whose indefatigable moral and financial support sustained our work every step along the way. We hope that this volume and the larger project of which it is a part can advance in some small way Brembeck's vision of a world free from the fear of nuclear war.

We owe special thanks to our colleagues at the Joan B. Kroc Institute for International Peace Studies. Raimo Väyrynen, Regan director of the Kroc Institute, was especially helpful, taking time from his busy schedule to offer insights and suggestions and agreeing to write the preface for this volume. His encouragement and support were indispensable to the success of this project. We are also grateful to our colleague George Lopez, who served as an advisor to the project, even while on sabbatical, and offered important advice and encouragement. We benefited greatly from the statistical expertise and research assistance of Jackie G. Smith, doctoral candidate in the Department of Government and International Studies at the University of Notre Dame. We express our thanks as well to Sandy Krizmanich and Abir Khater for their help in various administrative tasks.

The staff of the Fourth Freedom Forum provided substantial support for every phase of this project. Without their skillful and dedicated effort, this project would not have been possible. We are especially grateful to Jennifer Glick and Julia Wagler, who spent many long hours in the difficult and often thankless task of editing text and checking documentation. The polished quality of the text is a testament to their careful and highly professional editorial assistance. We are also grateful to Ann Miller Pedler and Miriam Redsecker for the crucial administrative support they provided. We thank Barbara Budgett for preparing the camera-ready copy.

This project benefited from an extraordinary group of advisors who helped shape our program and gave professional advice in framing the survey questionnaire. We owe a special thanks to Stephen P. Cohen, director of the Program in Arms Control, Disarmament, and International Security at the University of Illinois at Urbana-Champaign. Widely acknowledged as one of the leading North American experts on South Asia, Cohen generously gave of his time and expertise in providing invaluable guidance and support for this project. We received specialized assistance in the framing of the questionnaire from Neil Joeck of the Lawrence Livermore National Laboratory, Elaine El Assal of the United States Information Agency, P.R. Chari of the Centre for Policy Research in New Delhi, Ronald Hinckley of RSM Inc., Phil Oldenburg with Columbia University, Caroline Russell of the U.S. Arms Control and Disarmament Agency, Myron Weiner of the Massachusetts Institute of Technology, and Neeraj Kaushal, senior editor of *The Economic Times* in New Delhi. We are grateful for the assistance of Archana Jain-Gupta, the executive who coordinated the polling project on behalf of the Marketing and Research Group in New Delhi.

Last but not least, we owe an enormous debt of gratitude to our coauthors, Kanti Bajpai at Jawaharlal Nehru University, Sumit Ganguly of CUNY/Hunter College, Aabha Dixit of the Institute for Defence Studies and Analyses, and Varun Sahni of Jawaharlal Nehru University. The coauthors were prompt in meeting their deadlines, tolerant in accepting our editing suggestions, and enthusiastically supportive throughout.

We are grateful for the support and encouragement of so many gifted people. We take full responsibility for whatever errors or shortcomings this volume may have. We hope this study contributes to the realization of a safer and more secure future for South Asia and the world.

David Cortright and Amitabh Mattoo
Goshen, Indiana and New Delhi, India

About the Contributors

Kanti Bajpai is associate professor at the School of International Studies, Jawaharlal Nehru University, New Delhi. He is the author of *Interpreting World Politics* (1995).

David Cortright is the president of the Fourth Freedom Forum in Goshen, Indiana, and a visiting fellow at the Joan B. Kroc Institute for International Peace Studies at the University of Notre Dame. He is the author of *Peace Works: The Citizen's Role in Ending the Cold War* (1993).

Aabha Dixit is a research associate at the Institute for Defence Studies and Analyses, New Delhi, and is a columnist for several Indian newspapers.

Sumit Ganguly is professor of Political Science, Hunter College, City University of New York (CUNY). He is the author of *The Origins of War in South Asia: The Indo-Pakistani Conflicts Since 1947* (2d ed., 1994).

Amitabh Mattoo is an associate professor at the School of International Studies, Jawaharlal Nehru University. He is a former visiting fellow at the Joan B. Kroc Institute for International Peace Studies, and is the author of *The Politics of Protest: A Study of the Campaign for Nuclear Disarmament* (1995).

Varun Sahni is an associate professor at the School of International Studies, Jawaharlal Nehru University. He is currently editing a volume on war, peace, and the international system. He is the author of *Secure and Solvent: Thinking About an Affordable Defence for India* (1994).

Jackie G. Smith is a doctoral candidate in the Department of Government and International Studies at the University of Notre Dame. Her research focuses on the efforts of transnational nongovernmental organizations to influence political change in the areas of disarmament, development, and environmental protection.

Raimo Väyrynen is the John M. Regan Jr. director of the Joan B. Kroc Institute for International Peace Studies at the University of Notre Dame. He has published widely on issues of international security.

India and the Bomb

Indian Nuclear Policy Options

1

Indian Public Opinion and Nuclear Weapons Policy

David Cortright and Amitabh Mattoo

During the spring of 1990, at the peak of a major wave of insurgency in Kashmir, the Indian subcontinent may have come perilously close to the brink of nuclear war. According to Richard J. Kerr, then deputy director of the U.S. Central Intelligence Agency, it was the most dangerous nuclear confrontation he had seen during his many years of service with the U.S. government.[1] Kerr believes it was "far more frightening than the Cuban missile crisis," the closest the world has ever come to an actual nuclear exchange.[2] After American journalist Seymour Hersh broke the story in March 1993, top officials in both India and Pakistan denied that there had ever been such a crisis.[3] Just over two years later, however, in April 1995, a retired Indian official who had occupied a top government position during the 1990 crisis disclosed that the government of India had indeed taken seriously the possibility of a Pakistani nuclear strike and had even set up a task force to study the dimensions of this threat and recommend appropriate responses.[4] The last word on the 1990 crisis has not been written, and it will continue to provoke debate among academics and policymakers alike in the months to come. The incident illustrates, however, the potential dangers posed by the climate of nuclear suspicion and obfuscation that now exists on the subcontinent.

Overview

This study is an attempt to bring clarity to the Indian nuclear debate. It features a major new study of elite public opinion in India specially commissioned for this book. The results of the survey are combined with a series of essays that probes the various nuclear options facing New Delhi. The opinion survey asked not only what respondents were thinking about nuclear policy but also why they held such views.[5] It identifies the factors that shape public opinion and the considerations that might convince a respondent to think differently. A summary of the survey results is contained in this chapter. A complete report, with tabular data and a listing of questions asked, is included as an appendix.

This study addresses four crucial, but often neglected, questions. First, is India's nuclear policy consonant with the opinions of educated and influential elites? Second, do policies other than those articulated by the government of India have public—or at least elite—support? Third, what are the underlying factors that determine the views of Indian elites on the nuclear question? Finally, what are the factors that might influence elites to alter their opinions? The data collected with this survey provide important, sometimes unexpected, answers to these questions.

In the essays that follow this opening chapter we have asked four young authors to explore the pros and cons of the four major nuclear policy options facing India:

1. maintaining the present posture of nuclear ambiguity, i.e., neither overtly acquiring nor renouncing nuclear weapons,
2. renouncing the nuclear option and abstaining from any nuclear weapons development,
3. freezing the current levels of nuclear production and weapons development, and
4. acquiring an overt nuclear weapons capability and proceeding with outright weaponization.

In each of these essays the variations on these different options are thoroughly examined, providing a rich mosaic of analysis and information on the available options and the costs and benefits of each.

In chapter 2 Kanti Bajpai of Jawaharlal Nehru University examines the option of renouncing nuclear weapons. Bajpai identifies the different forms that nuclear abstinence could take—conditional or unconditional, bilateral with Pakistan or unilateral—and explores the arguments for and against each. Bajpai is not optimistic about the political feasibility of this option, given the meager support for nuclear opposition found in our opinion poll and the lack of an organized constituency on its behalf within Indian politics, but he nonetheless makes a convincing case for the strategic viability of renouncing the nuclear weapons option.

Aabha Dixit of the Institute for Defence Studies and Analyses focuses in chapter 3 on India's current policy of "strategic ambiguity." Dixit is clearly in sympathy with the government's policy and argues that New Delhi's position reflects a prudent mix of idealism and pragmatism. Dixit does not emphasize India's de facto nuclear capabilities or advanced weapons programs. Rather, her chapter examines in detail the historical evolution of India's nuclear policy, particularly the legacy of Gandhi and Nehru, and provides essential background to an understanding of the Indian nuclear debate.

In chapter 4 Sumit Ganguly, of City University/Hunter College in New York, locates the "nuclear freeze" option in the regional and international security environment. Ganguly argues that the signing of a comprehensive test ban treaty and a global ban on the production of fissile material would form the key components of a nuclear freeze in the region. As he points out, however, unless adequate verification mechanisms are put in place and some restraints are placed on the continued testing and development of ballistic missiles, the freeze option may lose its usefulness.

Varun Sahni, also of Jawaharlal Nehru University, writes in chapter 5 with considerable flair on the option of "going nuclear." Sahni examines four different postures within an overt nuclear weapons capability—nonweaponized, minimal, triad, and all horizons—and explains the potential military, political, economic, and environmental consequences of each. Sahni argues that the triad and all horizons postures would impose intolerable burdens on India. While the minimal and nonweaponized postures are more feasible, they too would pose risks and uncertainties for India's security.

Our perspective is frankly in line with the traditional disarmament posture, but we have tried to be objective in presenting the various options available to New Delhi. We have sought to identify the current state of public opinion on these issues and to examine the underlying motivations that might prompt different beliefs.

Democratizing the Nuclear Debate

One of the principal missions of this study is to democratize the nuclear debate in India. As in many other countries, the decisions about India's nuclear program are usually taken in secret by a few individuals.[6] India's vast nuclear establishment continues to function even today without any real public accountability. The chairman of India's Atomic Energy Commission, for instance, has the absolute power to "initiate, formulate, plan and execute India's nuclear program in total secrecy"[7] and is responsible only to the prime minister. Informed observers have referred to India's nuclear decision-making process as "scientific and political czarism,"[8] or as a virtual "nuclear sub-government."[9] Reasoned public discussion of nuclear policy options is almost entirely lacking in India, which otherwise has a rich and vibrant democratic tradition of dialogue and debate.[10] There is not much emphasis on nuclear policy in the media, in public forums, or in the two houses of Parliament—all of which seem otherwise preoccupied with domestic problems.[11] India's nuclear policy has never been an issue in general elections, and even among nongovernmental organizations, discussion of national security and nuclear issues is scarce.[12] Only a handful of antinuclear organizations exists in a country of nearly one billion people, and only rarely has there been any popular mobilization on the subject.[13] A small Delhi-based antinuclear weapons organization, Committee for a Sane Nuclear Policy, has attempted to build a constituency but without much success. Not surprisingly, therefore, little is known about the attitudes and preferences of India's intelligentsia on vital issues of nuclear policy.

There is, admittedly, a steady stream of articles on the subject in quasi-official journals and a few newspapers. But this discourse has been almost totally appropriated by a handful of scholars and former military and government officials who usually present no more than a justification of official policy. On sensitive subjects such as national security, the government can and often does restrict the availability of information, and even those given access to nuclear secrets are prevented from disseminating them through the special Atomic Energy Act of 1962 or the more pervasive Official Secrets Act. Under Section 18 (i) of the Atomic Energy Act, the government has the power to restrict the disclosure of information in any form that relates to an existing or proposed plant used for producing, developing, or using atomic energy. Through state patronage of research institutes and universities and the release of selected information to sympathetic investigators, the government is able to control much of the discussion that takes place on nuclear policy options. Our study, by commissioning an independent survey of elite opinion, seeks not only to explore current attitudes on the subject but to initiate a wider debate on India's nuclear options. Our hope is that this project will be only the beginning of a process that eventually leads to greater government openness and accountability on this vital issue.

Nuclear Ambiguity

This study is necessary, we believe, because of the apparent contradiction between New Delhi's posturing on the nuclear issue and its actual capability. On the one hand, India is and has been one of the leading advocates of global nuclear disarmament. This idealist tradition is deeply rooted in the legacy of Indian independence and the nonviolent movement led by Mohandas Karamchand Gandhi. The Mahatma was shocked by the atomic bombing of Hiroshima and Nagasaki and believed that the bomb would bring moral devastation on those who developed and used it. He vowed to fight for the outlawing of nuclear weapons. A Hindu extremist assassinated Gandhi in January 1948, shortly after India attained independence, and it was left to Gandhi's handpicked choice for leader,

Jawaharlal Nehru, India's first prime minister, to translate these ideas into policy. Nehru did so with remarkable finesse. He pioneered proposals for worldwide nuclear disarmament, including the idea of a nuclear test ban treaty and a freeze on the production of fissile material. These ideas later became part of the international arms control lexicon and are still debated today.[14] As early as 1954, in a message transmitted to the secretary general of the United Nations, Nehru suggested a "Standstill Agreement" to suspend the testing of nuclear weapons.[15] When India's Atomic Energy Commission was set up in 1948, just a year after independence, Nehru insisted to Parliament that the country's nuclear energy program would be for "the welfare of the people of India and other peaceful purposes." In 1957 he was even more explicit:

> No man can prophesy the future. But I should like to say on behalf of any future Government of India that whatever might happen, whatever the circumstances, we shall never use this atomic energy for evil purposes. There is no condition attached to this assurance, because once a condition is attached, the value of such an assurance does not go very far.[16]

The moral tone set by Nehru continued to influence India's nuclear policy even after his death. This was especially evident in New Delhi's position on the issue of nuclear nonproliferation. It is well known that India refused to sign the Nuclear Nonproliferation Treaty (NPT), arguing that the agreement discriminated between nuclear haves and have-nots. Less well known is the fact that India had proposed a treaty "To Prevent the Proliferation of Nuclear Weapons" in 1965, five years before the NPT was signed. The main provisions of the treaty offered by India were quite different from those incorporated into the NPT. The New Delhi draft sought an agreement that would (a) avoid any loopholes that might permit nuclear or nonnuclear powers to spread nuclear weapons capability in any form, (b) embody an acceptable balance of mutual responsibilities and obligations between the nuclear and nonnuclear states, (c) move a step further toward the achievement of general and complete disarmament and, more particularly, nuclear disarmament, and (d) include acceptable and workable provisions to ensure the effectiveness of the treaty.[17]

This idealistic posture persisted even after China tested its nuclear weapon in 1964, although then Indian prime minister Lal Bahadur Shastri's commitment to India's antinuclear posture seemed less steadfast than Nehru's.[18] From the 1970s into the 1990s India continued to campaign vigorously for global nuclear disarmament, consistently rejecting the doctrine of nuclear deterrence as "unethical and immoral." During the UN Second Special Session on Disarmament in 1982, Indian prime minister Indira Gandhi proposed a "Program of Action on Disarmament." At the

Third Special Session in 1988, her son, Prime Minister Rajiv Gandhi, tabled an "Action Plan for Ushering in a Nuclear-Weapon-Free and Non-Violent World Order" that attracted considerable international attention. In 1993 India cosponsored, with twenty-nine other countries including the United States, a resolution aimed at securing an early global ban on the production of fissile material for nuclear weapons or other nuclear explosive devices.[19] The moral theme of India's official nuclear policy has remained fixed on the following principles:

- A strong commitment to the peaceful uses of nuclear energy, and the development of a broad-based indigenous nuclear program;
- Rejection of the military uses of nuclear energy;
- Active support for the liberal pacifist critique of nuclear weapons and their attendant dangers;
- Emphasis on equity, fairness, and justice in the negotiation of international agreements on nuclear nonproliferation;[20]

In short, a commitment to peaceful uses of nuclear energy, non-weaponization, and global disarmament.

On the other hand, India's considerable nuclear capabilities and its advanced missile and aircraft programs are glaringly at odds with its official disarmament posture. India has developed, as part of its civilian nuclear energy program, one of the most sophisticated nuclear establishments in the world. India's nuclear estate is almost totally outside international safeguards and could easily be diverted to military uses. Of the ten nuclear power reactors that are currently operating or have been commissioned, only four are under International Atomic Energy Agency (IAEA) safeguards. None of the eight reactors under construction have any international safeguards. Similarly, none of the eight research reactors, including one Fast Breeder Test Reactor, are under IAEA scrutiny. India's two uranium enrichment plants and eight heavy water production facilities are also lacking safeguards.[21] India tested a nuclear device in 1974, and it has been estimated that the country has accumulated sufficient weapons-grade plutonium for about eighty nuclear weapons.[22] India possesses fixed-winged aircraft, including the British/French Jaguar and the Soviet-supplied MiG-23 and MiG-27, both of which can be modified to carry nuclear weapons. In October 1988, a well-known defense journal claimed that the Indian Defence Research and Development Organisation had been perfecting nuclear aerial bombing techniques using the MiG-23 and MiG-27 aircraft.[23] In addition, India has made significant advances in missile technology by successfully testing the *Prithvi*, a short-range missile with a range of 150–250 kilometers and the *Agni*, an intermediate-range ballistic missile with a range of about 2,500 kilometers.

There exists in India today an influential pro-bomb lobby that has the backing of at least a section of the government. Many of these nuclear hawks have worked for the government, still receive intelligence briefings, and are using the idiom of Western strategic thought to support their arguments in favor of India crossing the nuclear threshold. The doctrine of nuclear deterrence is an integral part of their world view. For these nuclear hawks, China, against whom India fought a war in 1962, poses a serious security threat, as does the possibility of a collusion between Beijing and Islamabad against New Delhi. Any regional deal to denuclearize South Asia, they believe, must include China as well as nuclear-capable Pakistan. A few of these former officials have even suggested, albeit off the record, that many of the disarmament proposals tabled by India in international fora were presented on the assumption that they would never be translated into reality.[24]

Some of these hawkish ideas are beginning to take root in official thinking and have been echoed more frequently in public following the May 1995 NPT extension conference. Some influential figures in the government privately agree with the realpolitik of the nuclear advocates, and New Delhi has shown less enthusiasm for the Comprehensive Test Ban Treaty (CTBT) and proposals for a worldwide freeze on the production of fissile material. India's most prominent nuclear advocate, former secretary of defence (production) K. Subrahmanyam—who still commands some influence in the government—has called on India's leaders to reverse their long-held positions on a test ban and fissile material cutoff:

> If it is to be taken seriously on . . . [nuclear] issues, India should announce in view of the legitimization of nuclear weapons by the international community [through the indefinite extension of the NPT] that it proposes to watch further developments carefully and will, therefore, abstain for the present from support to the comprehensive test ban treaty and the fissile materials cutoff.[25]

In a meeting in June 1995 with members of the Parliamentary Consultative Committee for Foreign Affairs, External Affairs Minister Pranab Mukherjee seemed to agree with Subrahmanyam, at least in part. Mukherjee reiterated that India will not sign the NPT because "it legalizes the nuclear arsenals of states already possessing large stockpiles of mass annihilation weapons," but he also said that India "will not unilaterally stop the production of fissionable material." He added cryptically that in contemporary conditions it was necessary to differentiate one's approach to the problem of producing fissionable materials, especially to their use.[26] India's principal opposition party, the Hindu-nationalist

Bharatiya Janata Party (BJP), has favored the country developing nuclear weapons for at least the last five years. Its president, L.K. Advani, has declared:

> I think we have no option in this regard, Pakistan having become nuclear, China having been nuclear for many years now, India, simply in order to have its dealings with these two neighbors on a level ground, must be nuclear.[27]

India clearly faces momentous choices on nuclear policy in the years ahead. We hope that this study sheds light on these issues and can help to bring about a more informed choice. In the pages that follow we describe our study method and review the findings of the Kroc Institute opinion survey.

The Survey Findings

Our survey of elite opinion on the nuclear issue was specially commissioned for this study. Marketing and Research Group Pvt. Ltd. of New Delhi, one of India's leading market research companies, conducted the survey between late September and early November 1994. A report of the findings was released in the U.S. and India in February 1995 and generated considerable interest and much debate.[28] The study method consisted of face-to-face interviews of approximately twenty to thirty minutes' duration with individual respondents in seven Indian cities. The target sample size was one thousand, with 992 responses. Less than 10 percent of the respondents were women.

The survey document divided respondents into three groups: (a) supporters of official policy, those who favor neither renouncing nuclear weapons nor acquiring them; (b) nuclear advocates, those supporting India's acquisition of nuclear weapons; and (c) nuclear opponents, those favoring renunciation of nuclear weapons. The survey probed the underlying motivations of current beliefs as well as the factors that might convince respondents to alter their opinions. Supporters of official policy were asked what would motivate them to advocate India's acquisition of nuclear weapons and what might convince them to renounce the nuclear option. Nuclear advocates were asked to identify their reasons for holding such a view and what considerations might lead them to back away from this position. Nuclear opponents were asked the reasons for their beliefs and what might induce them to change their minds. All three groups of respondents were asked to identify situations in which India might be justified in using nuclear weapons. All the respondents were also asked to indicate the extent of their support for an international treaty for the elimination of nuclear weapons, and if and when they believed such a treaty would be signed. Respondents' views on the NPT were also recorded.

The survey respondents were randomly selected from a cross section of educated elites representing a variety of professions: government civil service, academics, science, politics, law, journalism, medicine, business, armed forces, the police, sports, and the arts. Among those interviewed were secretaries of government departments, members of Parliament, university professors, heads of major laboratories, judges of the Supreme Court, retired and serving generals, and award-winning artists. Academicians, scientists, government officials, diplomats, journalists, and officers from the armed forces and the police accounted for 72 percent of the respondents. The decision to target educated elites was intentional. In a country where almost half of the population lacks formal education, knowledge of nuclear issues is extremely limited. While those in the Indian electorate, even the nonliterate, are politically conscious and turn out in considerable numbers for local and national elections, the nuclear issue has never been an issue in these elections and is not discussed in political campaigns. To test the support of official policy and explore preferences for a variety of sometimes complex policy alternatives, it was necessary to target educated elites. Moreover, this group is the most influential politically, and has the greatest potential to shape the course of government policy, although its existing influence on nuclear policy is clearly limited.

Six of the seven cities selected themselves. Bangalore, Bombay, Calcutta, Hyderabad, New Delhi, and Madras are all major metropolitan cities with populations of more than one million. They are all cities of influence and power. We decided to include Lucknow for two reasons. First, if only metropolitan cities were targeted, the regional balance would tip in favor of South India, whereas traditionally it has been the North, the so-called Hindi heartland, where the course of Indian politics is determined.[29] Second, Lucknow is the capital of India's largest state Uttar Pradesh, and as one of the principal centers of assertion by the economically and socially backward Hindu castes, is witnessing the emergence of a powerful new elite.

Our survey found substantial support for current government policy. Fifty-seven percent of those polled (N=563) favored New Delhi's policy of neither confirming nor denying a de facto nuclear capability while espousing global nuclear disarmament. Thirty-three percent (N=326) were nuclear advocates, favoring weaponization and the outright acquisition of nuclear weapons capability. Only 8 percent (N=83) supported the renunciation of a nuclear option for India.

Of the factors that would motivate respondents to favor or oppose a nuclear option for India, the two most important considerations were the perception of a nuclear threat from Pakistan and the possibility of a "time-bound plan for global nuclear disarmament." When supporters of government policy were asked what could justify India developing nuclear weapons, 52 percent cited threats from other nuclear powers and 48 percent identified a Pakistani nuclear test. By contrast, only 17 percent cited concerns about a possible deterioration in relations with China. Similarly, when nuclear advocates were asked why they favored the nuclear option, 57 percent identified threats from a nuclear Pakistan, with only 20 percent expressing concern about threats from China.

These findings are significant because they are at odds with pronouncements from New Delhi. Supporters of official policy have traditionally given substantial weight to the potential threat from China. Indeed it was the fear of Beijing, arising from the 1962 war and the subsequent nuclear test in 1964, that prompted some Indian officials to consider the nuclear option in the first place. And it is the continuing nuclear capability of China that motivates New Delhi's emphasis on the regional or triangular nuclear dilemma rather than any bilateral relationships with Pakistan. Our survey found, however, that elite opinion was concerned primarily with Pakistan. The potential threat from China did not register as a major consideration. The policy implications of this finding are potentially significant, as we shall explore in more detail below. A bilateral nuclear agreement with Pakistan would have political support among Indian elites and could reduce pressures for developing an overt nuclear capability.

Equally significant is the wide backing our study discovered for global nuclear disarmament. When supporters of official policy were asked what conditions would permit India to renounce a nuclear option, 58 percent cited a time-bound plan for global nuclear disarmament, with 26 percent citing a verifiable renunciation of Pakistan's nuclear option. When nuclear advocates were asked to identify the circumstances that would permit India to go without nuclear weapons, the largest group, 42 percent, cited a global ban on nuclear testing and development. Global solutions are taken very seriously in India and could have significant influence in obviating the perceived need for nuclear weapons capability. The decisions adopted by the major nuclear powers on international disarmament issues thus have significance beyond their borders and could substantially influence the prospects for denuclearization in South Asia.

The following are more detailed findings from the survey:

Regions. There were some differences in opinion across cities. Fewer nuclear opponents were found in Lucknow and Madras (3 percent and 5 percent respectively), while in Bombay and Calcutta the proportion of nuclear opponents was greater than the 8 percent overall average (13 percent and 12 percent respectively). Calcutta also had a significantly smaller proportion of nuclear advocates (22 percent versus 33 percent for all others). Otherwise, the differences among cities were not statistically significant. Systematic regional variations in nuclear policy opinion were not detected. A pooling of data across cities was thus permissible and yielded a fairly uniform pattern of national opinion on these issues.

Biographic Characteristics. Only slight variations were found in the views held by people in different occupational categories. Lawyers and business executives were more likely to be nuclear advocates, while members of the armed forces were less inclined to favor the nuclear option. Artists tended to be nuclear opponents. But these differences were small and insignificant. Men were less likely than women to be nuclear opponents, but the differences were slight and, as noted earlier, the sample of female respondents was small (a reflection of the male dominance in Indian elite society). There were no effects of age or education on respondents' positions.

Political Affiliation. No sizable correlation existed between political party affiliation and views on nuclear policy, although some slight differences were noted. Supporters of the Bharatiya Janata Party, the only national party that has publicly advocated the acquisition of nuclear weapons, were less inclined to be nuclear opponents and more likely to favor the nuclear option. Not surprisingly, supporters of the ruling Congress (I) were more likely to endorse official policy.

Salience. Only 6 percent of the respondents considered the nuclear issue sufficiently urgent to be rated the first- or second-most important concern facing the country. Communalism, poverty, economic stability, terrorism, the conflict in Kashmir, and even GATT ranked above the nuclear issue for most respondents. There was no sizable correlation between respondents' ranking of the nuclear issue and their views on the subject, although nuclear advocates were more likely to consider the question urgent. In response to a separate question, 41 percent of respondents considered the nuclear issue to be very important. Again, nuclear advocates were more likely to consider the issue urgent than the other two groups.

Availability of Information. Only 13 percent of the respondents felt that information on nuclear issues is easily available. A majority of the respondents (61 percent) believed that obtaining information on nuclear issues is either not easy or difficult. A significant correlation did not exist between views on nuclear policy and opinions on the availability of information.

Opinion on the Civilian Nuclear Energy Program. An overwhelming majority of respondents (87 percent) believed that civilian nuclear energy can help meet India's energy deficit. Nearly 60 percent felt that the benefits of a civilian nuclear energy program far outweigh its cost. However, more than 60 percent of the respondents agreed that a civilian nuclear program has high environmental costs attached. There was no significant correlation between views on nuclear weapons policy and attitudes toward the country's civilian nuclear energy program.

Circumstances Justifying Development of Nuclear Weapons. Each group of respondents—supporters of official policy, nuclear advocates, and nuclear opponents—were asked to identify conditions or reasons that would justify India becoming a nuclear weapons state. Among supporters of official policy, 52 percent cited threats from other nuclear powers, with 48 percent referring specifically to a Pakistani nuclear test. Few believed that a serious deterioration of relations with China (17 percent) or a breakdown of India's relations with the Western countries (12 percent) would justify weaponization. Thirteen percent of this group felt that no circumstances could justify the development of nuclear weapons.

Among nuclear advocates the primary justification for going nuclear was the perceived threat from a nuclear-capable Pakistan. Fifty-seven percent cited this concern. A slightly smaller percentage of this group believed that nuclear weapons could improve India's bargaining power in world affairs (49 percent), while 38 percent agreed with the view that nuclear weapons would enhance India's international status. Of less concern to nuclear advocates were threats from other nuclear powers (27 percent), threats from China (20 percent), or the prospect of increased international pressure on India's domestic policies (18 percent).

Among nuclear opponents, understandably, the vast majority (60 percent) asserted that no circumstances could justify India developing nuclear weapons. Of those willing to consider such an option, 22 percent cited threats from other nuclear powers and 10 percent identified a Pakistan nuclear test.

Circumstances Under Which Nuclear Weapons Could be Renounced. A majority of those supporting official policy (58 percent) would agree to renounce a nuclear option if the international community were to adopt a time-bound plan for global nuclear disarmament. Twenty-six percent would forgo the nuclear option in the event of a verifiable renunciation of Pakistan's nuclear capability. Only 15 percent believed that a final boundary settlement with China or the removal of Chinese nuclear weapons from Tibet would warrant such a move. Few would approve such a move in exchange for a seat on the UN Security Council (12 percent), guaranteed access to technology (9 percent), or diplomatic and political support for India's position on Kashmir (8 percent). Of the supporters of official policy, 18 percent would not favor renouncing the nuclear option under any circumstances.

Among nuclear advocates, 33 percent would never agree to renounce the nuclear option. Of those willing to consider such a possibility, 42 percent cited a global ban on nuclear testing and development as a justification for doing so. Another 18 percent mentioned a verifiable renunciation of Pakistan's nuclear option. Fewer would be motivated by a permanent seat on the Security Council (14 percent) or a final boundary settlement with China and removal of Chinese nuclear weapons from Tibet (10 percent).

Extent of Developing Nuclear Weapons. Nuclear advocates were asked to specify the scale of nuclear weapons development they would favor. Thirty-five percent were of the opinion that India should develop a nuclear arsenal capable of striking all nuclear powers in all directions, a *tous azimuths* policy. A smaller group, 19 percent, wanted India to develop an arsenal capable of striking only China and Pakistan, while 12 percent favored a capability directed against Pakistan alone. A substantial group, 34 percent, wanted to develop components of a nuclear program but not actually assemble any nuclear weapons.

The Potential Impact of Sanctions. Several questions were asked regarding the threat of international sanctions, to determine if this might be a factor influencing public opinion either for or against nuclear weapons development. This issue was included because of proposals that are sometimes offered in the West to use economic sanctions to pressure India into complying with nonproliferation policy objectives. The findings of our survey suggest that sanctions would have little or no effect on Indian attitudes. For supporters of official policy, increased international pressures would not influence them to support weaponization (only 18 percent believed that they would), and the threat of sanctions would not persuade them to renounce the nuclear option (only 7 percent cited this concern). Among nuclear advocates, international pressure on domestic policies was only a minor consideration in justifying weaponization (18 percent identified this factor) and was far less important than other considerations. Nor would advocates be convinced to renounce nuclear weapons by the threat of international sanctions. Only 8 percent cited this as a consideration for choosing not to acquire nuclear weapons.

The Possible Use Of Nuclear Weapons. Among all respondents—supporters of official policy, advocates, and opponents—44 percent felt that nuclear weapons could never be used under any circumstances. Among the group supporting official policy, 46 percent thought that these weapons could never be used. Of the official policy supporters willing to consider the use of nuclear weapons, 30 percent believed that India could employ these weapons if Pakistan were about to take over Kashmir. Twenty-five percent favored such use if a U.S.-led coalition of countries were to intervene militarily, while 24 percent believed that atomic weapons could be used if China were about to overwhelm India militarily.

Even among nuclear advocates, 33 percent felt that no circumstances could justify the actual use of nuclear weapons. For those willing to consider the option, the justification cited by the largest group, 45 percent, was the prospect of Pakistan about to take over Kashmir. Thirty percent believed that nuclear weapons could be used if a U.S.-led coalition of countries were to intervene militarily, while 26 percent cited the possibility of China overwhelming India militarily. Only 5 percent of nuclear advocates and an even smaller percentage of official policy supporters thought that nuclear weapons use would occur accidently.

Views on Arms Control Issues. No arms control issue has generated more concern and controversy in India than the Nuclear Nonproliferation Treaty. As noted above, New Delhi was an early advocate of a nonproliferation agreement, but it refused to sign the NPT in 1970 and has maintained a consistently hard line against the treaty ever since. India condemned the indefinite extension of the NPT in May 1995 at the UN Nuclear Nonproliferation Treaty Extension/Review Conference as reinforcing an unjust system of international nuclear inequality. Thus it came as something of a surprise in our survey to discover a considerable amount of conditional support for the NPT among Indian elites. While only 13 percent of all respondents favored India acceding to the treaty unilaterally, support for the NPT rose to 39 percent when the condition of Pakistan signing the treaty was added. Among supporters of official policy, 43 percent would sign the NPT either unilaterally or bilaterally. Among nuclear advocates, the comparable figure was 32 percent, while among nuclear opponents it was 54 percent. This support for bilateral accession to the NPT is potentially significant. Islamabad has declared that it will sign the treaty if New Delhi will do the same. The survey findings suggest that many Indian elites would favor this approach. This gives added weight to proposals for emphasizing bilateral relations between India and Pakistan as the key to defusing nuclear tensions in South Asia.

The idea of global nuclear disarmament has immense legitimacy and support among Indian elites. For all respondents, a whopping 92 percent expressed total or partial support for an international agreement to ban nuclear weapons, with only 3 percent opposed. Among supporters of official policy, 88 percent indicated total support for the elimination of nuclear weapons, with an additional 9 percent expressing partial support, for a combined 97 percent endorsement of nuclear abolition. Among nuclear advocates as well, support for a nuclear ban was widespread, with 91 percent indicating full or partial support for a global disarmament agreement. Respondents also expressed confidence in the feasibility of such an agreement, with 62 percent of all respondents believing that a global ban could be signed within 25 years. Among supporters of official policy, 65 percent felt that an elimination treaty could be signed within this timeline. Fifty-three percent of nuclear advocates agreed. Among nuclear opponents, 80 percent considered a nuclear ban feasible within 25 years.

Nuclear Opponents: Reasons for Renunciation. Despite the nonviolent tradition of Gandhi and the disarmament legacy of Nehru, opponents of a nuclear option for India were a small portion of our sample, just 8 percent. The reasons for their opposition were primarily moral and environmental rather than political. When asked why they opposed the nuclear option, 46 percent of this group agreed that nuclear weapons are morally repugnant. Forty-one percent cited the fact that nuclear production harms the environment, while 34 percent expressed concern that India cannot afford nuclear weapons. Twenty-nine percent agreed that nuclear weapons do not address the primary threats to India's security, i.e., terrorism and insurgency. Only 18 percent expressed concern that a nuclear India could become the target of the major powers. It should be noted that while only 8 percent of those in our sample identified themselves as opposed to a nuclear option, nearly half of all respondents, including a sizable portion of nuclear advocates, believed that the use of nuclear weapons could not be justified under any circumstances. Many were apparently willing to consider the nuclear option for political reasons but could not conceive of their actual use in military conflict.

Implications

For the government of India, the findings of our survey appear at first glance to offer some encouragement. A clear majority of educated elites expressed support for New Delhi's official policy of neither renouncing nor acquiring nuclear weapons while espousing global disarmament. But this declared support for official policy seemed quite shallow. The nuclear issue ranked very low in salience (seventh out of the ten issues considered), and most respondents agreed that information is either unavailable or difficult to obtain. This suggests that few Indians have strong opinions on the nuclear issue, and that the majority could be persuaded by new information or changing circumstances. A wider, more informed, and more critical public debate in India could lead to significant shifts in opinion.

Our study shows unmistakably that the perceived nuclear threat from Pakistan was the single most important factor motivating Indian elites to consider the nuclear option. The evidence suggests that Indian elites would strongly favor the acquisition of nuclear weapons if Pakistan were to test a nuclear device. A majority of nuclear advocates identified the threat from Pakistan as the reason India should develop nuclear weapons. A near majority of official policy supporters and even 10 percent of nuclear opponents also believed that India would be justified in developing nuclear weapons in the event of a Pakistani nuclear test. By comparison, threats from China or even a serious deterioration of relations with Beijing were not seen as justifying the development of nuclear weapons.

It is ironic that the threat which originally motivated New Delhi's consideration of a nuclear option has now faded from public consciousness, while a new Pakistani threat, largely created in response to India's capability, has become the primary motivation for continued consideration of that option. The nuclear arms competition in South Asia has thus become self-perpetuating. New Delhi created a nuclear capability in response to Beijing's program, which prompted Islamabad to match India's effort, which now provides motivation for New Delhi to maintain its program. Arms control diplomacy has become similarly circular, and self-defeating. Pakistan has offered to sign the NPT with India and enter into bilateral negotiations, but New Delhi insists on a regional approach that includes China. For its part, Beijing asserts that a regional arrangement is impossible without a broader international settlement, thus scuttling India's initiatives and sending the discussions back to square one. Many arms control experts have concluded from this that a regional approach is unworkable, and that the best hope for constraining the incipient arms race in South Asia is to call for direct bilateral arrangements between India and Pakistan. Our survey lends political legitimacy to this approach by demonstrating the overwhelming importance Indian elites attach to the perceived threat from Pakistan and by showing their widespread receptivity to bilateral denuclearization.

This was evident in the sizable constituency in favor of signing the NPT with Pakistan. While a majority of respondents were opposed to the NPT, 39 percent expressed a willingness to accede to the treaty either unilaterally or bilaterally with Pakistan. This support seems to reinforce the fact that Indian elites have a deep faith in the arms control process and that a CTBT and a treaty to freeze the production of fissile material would be greeted enthusiastically by most sections of the Indian elite.

This study has clearly identified two major factors that could convince Indian elites to forgo the nuclear option. The first would be a verifiable renunciation of Pakistan's nuclear option, the second a time-bound plan for global nuclear disarmament. Other factors, such as a final boundary settlement with China and the removal of Chinese nuclear weapons from Tibet, had little influence on opinion. The implications of the first point are obvious in confirming the importance of bilateral arms control with Islamabad. The second factor, support for global disarmament, points to both the responsibility and the opportunity the United States and the other nuclear powers have to influence events in South Asia. As the survey results indicate, Indian elites take the idea of nuclear disarmament very seriously. Respondents not only favored a nuclear ban, but many considered negotiation of such an agreement feasible within 25 years. A commitment by the major powers to negotiate for nuclear weapons elimination could have a decisive impact in persuading Indian public opinion to forgo the nuclear option.

Notes

1. Seymour Hersh, "On The Nuclear Edge," *The New Yorker*, March 29, 1993, 56–73.

2. Ibid., 56.

3. See, for instance, interview with then Chief of the Indian army, General V.N. Sharma, in *Economic Times* (New Delhi), 18 May 1993. According to Sharma, a nuclear threat by Pakistan was neither perceived by India nor conveyed to New Delhi by U.S. emissaries. A study carried out by the Henry L. Stimson Center in Washington, D.C. also came to the conclusion that the "threat of a nuclear confrontation was not great, nor were India and Pakistan eager to have another conventional war." See Michael Krepon and Mishi Faruqee, eds., *Conflict Prevention and Confidence-Building Measures in South Asia: The 1990 Crisis*, Washington, D.C., The Henry L. Stimson Center, Occasional Paper No. 17, April 1994.

4. This officer of unassailable credibility made the disclosure off the record. One of the authors of this chapter was present during the meeting. See Kanti Bajpai and Amitabh Mattoo, "First Strike!" *Pioneer* (New Delhi), 23 April 1995. According to Hersh's account, the crisis was diffused after Robert Gates, deputy U.S. national security advisor, flew on behalf of President Bush to Islamabad and New Delhi and negotiated a stand-down between the two countries. See Hersh, "On the Nuclear Edge," 56.

5. A few opinion surveys of Indian elites were carried out in the 1960s and early 1970s, but few comparable studies have been conducted since the Indian nuclear test in 1974. An important study was undertaken by a prominent Indian social-psychologist, Ashis Nandy, as part of the larger study, "Indian Elite Attitudes Toward the World of the 1990s and Particularly Towards Participation in a Possible Future World Order." See Ashis Nandy, "The Bomb, the NPT, and Indian Elites," *Economic and Political Weekly* (Bombay), Special Number, August 1982, 1533–40.

6. For an insightful study of India's nuclear decision making see Ashok Kapur, *India's Nuclear Option: Atomic Diplomacy and Decision Making* (New York: Praeger, 1976). Also see Onkar Marwah, "India's Nuclear and Space Programs: Intent and Policy," *International Security* 2, no. 2 (Fall 1977) 96–121, and Ziba Moshaver, *Nuclear Weapons Proliferation in the Indian Subcontinent* (New York: St. Martin's Press, 1991).

7. Dhirendra Sharma, *India's Nuclear Estate* (New Delhi: Lancers, 1983), 149.

8. Kapur, *India's Nuclear Option*, vii.

9. Sharma, *India's Nuclear Estate*, 2. See also Achin Vanaik and Praful Bidwai, "India and Pakistan," in *Security With Nuclear Weapons*? ed. Regina Cowen Carp (Oxford: SIPRI/Oxford Univ. Press, 1991). Vanaik and Bidwai are two prominent nuclear dissenters.

10. Perhaps the only real debate on India's nuclear options took place in the months after China tested its nuclear device in 1964. Distinguished economists, political leaders, and social activists participated in the discussion. The most insightful analysis was presented by Raj Krishna, a noted Indian economist, who suggested that there were four choices facing India: continuing with existing policy; aligning with the United States; establishing an independent deterrent; and formulating an 'optimum' defense policy. See Raj Krishna, "India and the Bomb," *India Quarterly* 21, no. 2 (April–June 1965): 119–37. Also see Jayaprakash Narain, "India, China and Peace," *Anarchy* 4, no. 8 (August 1964): 250–54, and "India and the Bomb: A Symposium," *Gandhi Marg* 10, no. 1 (January 1966): 11–18.

11. An exception was the minor political storm witnessed in the Indian Parliament in April 1994, when a news report revealed that a team of Indian officials held "secret" talks on the nuclear issue with a U.S. delegation led by Robert Einhorn, deputy assistant secretary of state. Members of Parliament from the opposition parties claimed that the government was bending to U.S. pressure to cap its nuclear program. The government denied these allegations, and soon enough the storm passed.

12. The lack of debate and serious thinking on the nuclear issue has caused concern not just to nuclear doves. K. Subrahmanyam, a former secretary of defence (production) in the government of India and best known of India's nuclear hawks, argues: "As a consistent advocate of the nuclear option for India for the last quarter of a century and as a person very familiar with the general thinking at the top levels of military and bureaucratic leadership, though not privy to their secrets, I despair whether the Indian establishment can be persuaded to apply their mind at all to a nuclear strategic policy . . . [India's] approach to security issues is purely reactive and *ad hocist* . . ." K. Subrahmanyam, "Nuclear Policy, Arms Control and Military Cooperation," paper presented at a conference on "India and the United States After the Cold War," sponsored by the India International Centre and Carnegie Endowment for International Peace, New Delhi, 7–9 March 1993.

13. Most of these organizations have campaigned only against India's civil nuclear energy program. Many of the country's nuclear plants are widely believed to operate below international safety standards. The campaigns against the proposed Kaiga atomic power plant in the Indian state of Karnataka and the existing Narora I and II plants in Uttar Pradesh have attracted media attention. India's most serious nuclear accident is said to have occurred on 31 March 1993 when fire raged for twelve hours inside Narora I's turbine generator unit disabling the reactor's primary and secondary cooling system. A backup cooling system was able to carry away the heat from the reactor core and prevent a meltdown. See "South Asia Nuclear Weapons Free Zone," *The Arms Control Reporter*, April 1993, 454.

14. At the Nuclear Nonproliferation Treaty Extension/Review Conference in May 1995, the nuclear powers specifically committed themselves to negotiating a comprehensive test ban treaty no later than 1996 and vowed "early conclusion of negotiations on a non-discriminatory and universally applicable convention banning the production of fissile material for nuclear weapons." Reprinted in "Documents: Resolutions Adopted at the NPT Extension Conference," *Arms Control Today* 25, no. 5 (June 1995): 30.

15. For details of India's disarmament proposals, see Government of India, *Disarmament: India's Initiatives*, External Publicity Division, Ministry of External Affairs, New Delhi, 1988.

16. Nehru made the statement while speaking at the inauguration of Apsara, India's first nuclear reactor, at Trombay (near Bombay) on 20 January 1957.

17. See Government of India, *Disarmament: India's Initiatives*.

18. Intervening in a debate on nuclear policy in the Indian Parliament in November 1964, only a month after China tested its first nuclear weapon, Shastri said, "I cannot say that the present policy [not to build a nuclear weapon] is deep-rooted, that it cannot be set aside, that it can never be changed. . . . An individual may have a certain static policy . . . but in the political field we cannot do so. . . . If there is need to amend what we have said today, then we will say, all right, let us go ahead and do so." It is believed that Homi J. Bhabha, the founder of India's nuclear program, received the approval of Shastri to work on a nuclear weapons option.

19. United Nations General Assembly, 48th Session, Resolution 48/75L, 16 December 1994.

20. C. Raja Mohan, "India's Nuclear Policy at the Crossroads," in *The Director's Series on Proliferation*, ed. Kathleen C. Bailey (California: Lawrence Livermore National Laboratory, 1993), 22.

21. For details of India's nuclear facilities see Leonard S. Spector and Mark G. McDonough, with Evan S. Medeiros, *Tracking Nuclear Proliferation, A Guide in Maps and Charts, 1995* (Washington, D.C.: Carnegie Endowment for International Peace, 1995).

22.

Indian Stockpile of Plutonium	1995
Production in Kilograms	
Cirus Reactor	280
Dhruva Reactor	190
CANDU (first discharges)	30
Total Production	**500**
Consumption in Kilograms	
1974 Test (Pokhran)	10
Processing Losses (3%)	15
Fast Breeder Reactor	50
Total Consumption	**75**
Net Stock	**425**

Source: David Albright et al., *World Inventory of Plutonium and Highly Enriched Uranium* (Oxford: SIPRI/Oxford Univ. Press, 1992).

23. *Defence and Foreign Affairs Weekly*, October 1988. See also Leonard S. Spector with Jacqueline R. Smith, *Nuclear Ambitions: The Spread of Nuclear Weapons 1989–90* (Boulder, Colo.: Westview, 1990).

24. This view was expressed by a former Indian foreign secretary at a seminar in New Delhi in January 1995.

25. K. Subrahmanyam, "Indefinite NPT Extension: India Must Formulate Response," *The Times of India* (New Delhi), 7 June 1995.

26. Yuri Kozmin's report for *Tass* from New Delhi, 28 June 1995.

27. "Interview with L.K. Advani," *The Economic Times* (New Delhi), 17 April 1993, 3.

28. See, for instance, Sunil Adam, "Sizable Section of India's Elite for Signing NPT," *Pioneer* (New Delhi), 11 February 1995; Pranay Sharma, "Pak Main Factor in Nuclear Option: Elite Voice Opinion in MARG Poll," *The Telegraph* (Calcutta), 6 February 1995; K. Subrahmanyam, "The People's Voice," *Economic Times* (New Delhi), 18 February 1995.

29. Bangalore, Hyderabad, and Madras are all in the southern part of India.

2

Abstaining: the Nonnuclear Option

Kanti Bajpai

The dictionary defines abstinence as choosing not to do something that is within one's power or to give up a resource one possesses. Thus, nuclear abstinence or renunciation would be a clear-sighted decision not to maintain any kind of nuclear weapons posture—not to go nuclear and not to keep the option open—when there is the capacity to do so. Apparently, this is India's least-preferred nuclear choice. Most Indian elites seem to prefer going nuclear or keeping the option open. The Kroc Institute poll showed that out of roughly one thousand elite respondents only 8 percent were abstainers. On the other hand, 57 percent wanted India to keep the option open and 33 percent favored going nuclear. At the same time, a plurality (44 percent) of all respondents to the Kroc Institute survey believed that there were no circumstances that would justify India's use of nuclear weapons. In response to the question, When could India use nuclear weapons? even one-third of those advocating nuclear weapons development cited *never* as the appropriate answer. Skepticism about the utility of nuclear weapons was widespread, despite the lack of overt support for renouncing this option. While abstinence was a distinctly minority position, there are good arguments supporting this nuclear choice.

Four Forms of Abstinence

Nuclear abstinence—and its synonym, nuclear renunciation—implies at least that India publicly announces its decision not to produce weapons now or in the foreseeable future; that, to the extent it has the resources and capabilities to produce weapons, it discloses them, opens them to inspection, and then verifiably divests itself of them; and that it permits ongoing inspections as a reassurance that nuclear weapons will not be produced clandestinely. Abstinence can be *conditional* or *unconditional*, *bilateral* or *unilateral*. It can therefore take the following forms: *conditionally bilateral, conditionally unilateral, unconditionally bilateral,* and *unconditionally unilateral*. Unilateral abstinence refers to a solely Indian decision to renounce nuclear weapons. Bilateral abstinence is used here to refer to an India/Pakistan agreement. It does not refer to an India/China agreement. This is because Pakistan has repeatedly stated that it would give up the nuclear option if India agreed to do so, while China has made no such statement. An India/Pakistan bilateral solution is therefore within India's power to choose; an India/China solution is not.

Abstinence would be *conditionally bilateral* if India's decision not to produce nuclear weapons, conjointly with a Pakistani commitment not to do so, depended minimally on two actions by the nuclear powers: a credible guarantee of protection against nuclear threats, and a promise of complete nuclear disarmament within some clearly defined period. By contrast, abstinence would be *conditionally unilateral* if India tied renunciation to nuclear protection and phased disarmament, irrespective of Pakistani actions. Because global disarmament must include in its ambit a near-nuclear or nuclear Pakistan, conditional bilateralism and conditional unilateralism are in the end not far apart. Conditional abstinence, bilateral or unilateral, might also be qualified by the right to resume a nuclear weapons program if the conditions under which it was originally undertaken were violated or if India's security experienced serious deterioration. Abstinence would be *unconditionally bilateral* if India agreed, along with a similar agreement from Pakistan, not to produce nuclear weapons while attaching no conditions to the behavior of the international community. If India renounced nuclear weapons despite Pakistani actions and the actions of the international community, abstinence would be *unconditionally unilateral*.

Nuclear Abstinence: Opponents and Proponents

Elite policy and popular opinion vary in the nature of their opposition to nuclear abstinence. There are those who see abstinence as born of military ignorance or naïveté: in a nuclearized world, abstinence is to invite aggression and intimidation. In the Kroc Institute survey, a majority (52 percent) of those supporting India's current policy cited threats from other nuclear powers as a justification for India's development of nuclear weapons. Moreover, when the ultimate currency of international power and status is a nuclear weapon, to be abstinent is to remain weak and second-rank. If so, going nuclear, or keeping the option open, makes military and diplomatic sense.

Others see abstinence as treasonous, cowardly, and luddite: to abstain is to play the game of India's enemies; it is to bend before the Western powers; and it is to revert to the psychology of technological stagnation and passivity which caused India to lose its independence to militarily superior powers in the eighteenth century (and, in more extreme versions, centuries earlier to other invaders). Going nuclear or keeping the option open, in this view, is a matter of political self-assertion and self-affirmation. Nearly half (49 percent) of the respondents to the Kroc Institute survey who favored nuclear weapons development did so because they felt it would improve India's bargaining power in world affairs.

Finally, still others see abstinence as irrational in an economic sense. According to the "more bang for the buck" argument, nuclear weapons are less expensive than conventional weapons and therefore are investments in affordable defense. In sum, the case against abstinence combines military, diplomatic, political, and economic arguments.

While the case against abstinence predominates, there have been periods in recent history when some form of abstinence had greater support. As late as the period from 1966 to 1968, as India considered whether to sign the Nuclear Nonproliferation Treaty (NPT), there was support for abstinence if the nuclear powers were prepared to defend the country against nuclear threats.[1] When it became clear that there was no prospect of obtaining a nuclear umbrella, support for the umbrella and for abstinence ended.

Since then there has been virtually no support for an umbrella or for any form of abstinence—with a few exceptions. One notable but little-known exception is the support for nuclear abstinence that has existed among some members of the armed forces. While this position has eroded since India's nuclear test in 1974, there remain a few small pockets of military support for abstinence on strategic grounds. Within the armed forces, sections of the army have worried that the navy and air force would gain prestige and resources if India went nuclear. A 1966 private survey of military officers of the rank of Lieutenant Colonel and above found these officials "uniformly opposed to the development of nuclear weapons."[2] As late as 1981, there were sections of the military opposed to nuclearization. Strategically, the armed forces have at various times seen the development of a nuclear option as detracting from preparedness at the conventional level.[3]

Nuclear abstinence has also been supported by some sections of the scientific community. Scientists outside the nuclear establishment have resented the relative neglect of other areas of research and development.[4] Support also exists within the nuclear establishment, although little is known about its size or rationale.[5] Nuclear abstinence is clearly the position of Gandhians, who support it on moral grounds. Forty-six percent of nuclear opponents in the Kroc Institute survey cited moral repugnance to such weapons as the reason India should renounce them. Gandhians believe that the development of weapons of mass destruction could never fit within the Mahatma's strict philosophy of absolute nonviolence. Abstinence is also supported by some socialists who, on economic and ecological grounds, argue for an unconditional bilateral agreement that would have India and Pakistan simultaneously agree not to produce weapons. Seventy-five percent of nuclear opponents cited economic and ecological reasons for forgoing nuclear weapons. The Gandhians and socialists would urge the nuclear weapons states to disarm within some stipulated period, but they would not make this the condition of an India/Pakistan agreement. Neither the Gandhians nor socialists advocate that India sign the NPT, which both regard as discriminatory.

Finally, antinuclearism manifests itself in two potentially larger movements that are more recent and more vigorous than the Gandhians and socialists, namely, women's groups and environmental groups. There are many internal differences within the women's and environmental movements, but there are sectors within each that oppose nuclear weapons. It should be noted that on a variety of issues these groups have shown an interest in and capacity for cooperation among themselves, and with others, such as the Gandhians and socialists.[6] This coalition may recall elements of the antinuclear and peace coalitions in other settings, specifically the United States and Western Europe in the 1980s.[7]

While there is little outright support for nuclear abstinence, it is worth examining this option in detail. If there is to be a thorough, rational nuclear debate in India, a dispassionate appraisal of the case for and against abstinence must be attempted. Few today are willing to make a case for nuclear abstinence. Ranged against supporters of abstinence are both the supporters of official policy and the nuclear advocates. Both have deployed strong arguments. If the abstainers are to be credible, they must counter these arguments. The case for abstinence in such a situation is better articulated by a dialectical "negation of the negation"—by stating not only the military, diplomatic, political, and economic, but also the ethical and technical arguments for and against the various forms of abstinence, then by presenting counterarguments for and against.

Conditional Abstinence
A Nuclear Umbrella and Phased Global Disarmament

Conditional abstinence, bilateral or unilateral, based on a nuclear umbrella and a phased process of global nuclear disarmament, has several advantages. A guarantee of nuclear protection would serve to stabilize a bilateral India/Pakistan agreement. It would be insurance against cheating by either side and a break out from abstinence. In addition, if India were guaranteed nuclear protection by the nuclear powers against all nuclear threats, this would counter both Pakistani and Chinese intimida-

Abstaining: the Nonnuclear Option 27

tion in a situation where India alone had abstained. A process of phased global disarmament would strengthen an India/Pakistan abstinence agreement by eliminating India's fear of Chinese nuclear weapons. It would also eliminate Pakistan's nuclear advantage over a unilaterally abstinent India. However, there are strong arguments against abstinence tied to an umbrella or phased disarmament.

A Nuclear Umbrella

The case against conditional abstinence rests first on the implausibility and undesirability of a nuclear umbrella. As India learned in the period of 1966 to 1968, the nuclear powers are extremely reluctant to extend their nuclear responsibilities beyond their own frontiers and the frontiers of their key allies. Even with respect to their close allies, the credibility of "extended deterrence" has often been in doubt. At least one reason the U.S. maintained conventional forces in Europe after 1945 was to reassure its allies that in case of conventional or nuclear attack, Washington would not be able to stand aside.

Opponents of abstinence would argue that there is no reason to suppose that after the cold war the chances of obtaining a nuclear umbrella have increased. What was true during the cold war remains true today: A nuclear umbrella could be manipulated. Under the protection of an umbrella, a mischievous nonnuclear power might be tempted to tease and provoke a nuclear antagonist. A nuclear protector might thus be dragged into another's conflict, and possibly even supervene the original dispute, leaving the agent provocateur watching on the sidelines as nuclear powers take one another on. Indeed, the agent provocateur might see the resulting conflict between nuclear powers as serving its interest. Mutual destruction might be perceived, if mistakenly, to leave the field clear for the instigator.[8]

Even if a nuclear umbrella might plausibly be obtained, doubts over the credibility of protection would render it undesirable. Those under its protection would constantly be tempted to develop their own deterrents. In addition, to accept nuclear protection would be highly fraught, diplomatically and politically, because to rely on another's protection would be to accept permanent second-rank status and to lose one's foreign policy autonomy. Finally, by insisting on a protective umbrella, one principal advantage of unilateral abstinence would be lost: If India chooses abstinence without an umbrella, Pakistan would be constrained to follow suit (a point to be argued later). However, in response to an umbrella, Islamabad might be induced to increase the scope of its program.

Against this it might be argued that with the end of the East/West confrontation, strategic dynamics have changed radically. In the interest of nonproliferation, the nuclear powers could offer a nuclear umbrella to countries such as India and Pakistan. Pran Chopra suggests that the international control of nuclear weapons and materials, as envisaged in the Baruch Plan, is realizable as never before. Nuclear collective security, guaranteed by an international authority such as the United Nations, is no longer utopian.[9]

However, both arguments are problematic. If recent events in the former Yugoslavia, former Soviet Union, and the Korean peninsula are any guide, there will continue to be areas where the U.S., Russia, and China have differing interests. Conscious of this, the big three, and the U.K. and France, will resist nuclear guarantees. The reluctance to commit themselves will also arise from a fear of nuclear overextension. Guarantees to India and Pakistan might prompt calls for protection from Argentina, Brazil, Israel, Kazakhstan, North Korea, the Ukraine, and so on to the nth country. In short, the answer to the nth country problem, that is, a chain of successive proliferators, is not the nth country solution.

As to the creation of an international nuclear authority—a super International Atomic Energy Agency (IAEA) with a monopoly of nuclear weapons—this confronts the problem of location and therefore of command and control. Nuclear weapons must *reside* somewhere. To be credibly under the management of a super IAEA, the weapons must in all likelihood reside in some neutral site. Otherwise, there will always be concern about who will truly be in command and control, especially at a critical moment. But in a world parceled out in nation-states, jealous of their territories and sovereignties, there are no vacant and neutral sites left to allocate to a supranational authority. Lacking such a space, the weapons could perhaps reside in the territory of the nuclear powers, yet not be activated without authenticated electronic signals from an international authority. However, one can imagine all types of dangerous situations arising from this divorce of authority and placement.

Richard Garwin has suggested that a modest international nuclear force be placed under the authority of the United Nations.[10] After a process of deep reductions by the nuclear powers, a nuclear command-and-control apparatus would be developed at the United Nations, perhaps under the authority of Article 43 of the UN Charter, which provides for a Military Staff Committee. Once this was established, the nuclear powers would transfer their remaining weapons to the UN authority. Francesco Calogero has criticized this proposal as impractical and ethically questionable.[11] The difficulties of deciding who would have command of the weapons and where they should be located would undermine the credibility of the proposed system. Moreover, it is inconsistent to argue that nuclear weapons are unnecessary while simultaneously proposing a continuation of nuclear deterrence, however limited. The idea of an international nuclear force is not likely to be militarily convincing or politically acceptable.

Phased Global Disarmament

Abstinence could also be tied to the promise of global nuclear disarmament (which would include the disarming of a nuclear Pakistan). This is consonant with India's present nuclear policy, and few if any Indians would be opposed. In the Kroc Institute survey, 83 percent of all respondents and 76 percent of respondents favoring the development of nuclear weapons cited an international agreement for the elimination of nuclear weapons as a condition under which India could renounce nuclear weapons. However, as things stand, there is little prospect that the nuclear powers, especially the U.S. and Russia, will promise to disarm in phases (say by 2010, as proposed by Indian prime minister Rajiv Gandhi at the UN in June 1988).[12] France and the U.K. are in some respects even more reluctant than the U.S. to forgo nuclear weapons. The U.S. and Russia have made sizable reductions in nuclear stockpiles, and they and their nuclear partners faced considerable pressure to eliminate nuclear weapons at the NPT Extension/Review Conference in New York in April/May 1995, but there is no evidence that the nuclear powers intend to negotiate for complete disarmament.

The reluctance of the major nuclear powers rests on several factors.[13] The military establishments of the U.S. and Russia remain convinced that nuclear weapons are necessary for their security—against each other's nuclear weapons and against states who have or might gain access to weapons of mass destruction. For both, a nuclear weapon remains a symbol of international status, however loath they are to admit this publicly. There are also technical and economic problems. To dismantle tens of thousands of weapons; to collect, transport, and detoxify the fissile material; to verify each other's cuts; to decommission idle nuclear plants; and to repair the environmental damage caused by half a century's nuclear weapons development: all these activities will stretch scientific and engineering capacities. A thoroughgoing disarmament process will also be financially burdensome, and, in the present economic circumstances, the legislatures of the two countries will find it difficult to allocate the requisite funding.[14]

Clearly, as long as the U.S. and Russia are armed, it is improbable that any of the other nuclear powers will disarm—especially, with regard to New Delhi's concerns, China. China continues to conduct nuclear tests, even as it hints that it might eventually join a comprehensive test ban CTB); and it repeats that it will not countenance arms control or disarmament talks until there is some degree of equivalence among all the nuclear powers.[15]

In sum, a nuclear umbrella is unlikely to be given and is just as unlikely to be sought or relied on for very long. On the other hand, abstinence on condition of global disarmament risks being construed as mere diplomatic maneuver—an offer made in the fullest expectation that it will be refused (as various Pakistani proposals for a bilateral nuclear agreement have been construed in New Delhi).

The Kroc Institute poll showed that the Indian elites prefer disarmament to protection. Nuclear protection rated only 6 percent and 4 percent support among those who want to keep the option open and those who would go nuclear, respectively. However, among those who wish to keep the option open, 58 percent supported abstinence on the promise of phased global disarmament, as would 42 percent of those who want to go nuclear. Clearly, a plan for negotiated worldwide reductions leading to the eventual elimination of nuclear weapons would have the greatest effect in increasing support for nuclear abstinence.

Unconditional Abstinence: The NPT or a Regional Deal

India could choose abstinence within a bilateral agreement and with no conditions attached to the behavior of third parties. It could do so by acceding with Pakistan to the NPT or by means of a regional arrangement. Both mechanisms have been publicly affirmed and accepted by Pakistan on various occasions and categorically rejected by India.

Three Arguments Against the NPT

The case against the NPT route is mostly ethical, diplomatic, and political. Increasingly, the objections to it and to a regional deal are also technical. First, since the inception of the treaty in 1968, New Delhi has opposed it as contrary to the norms of international society because it imposes unequal obligations on signatories. While the nonnuclear weapons powers are asked to renounce the option and to open their facilities to international inspection, the nuclear weapons powers are not constrained to dismantle their arsenals or to submit to any form of international scrutiny. India's formal position therefore is that, despite the nuclear test of 1974, it has neither exercised the nuclear option nor closed it.

Second, it is argued that no Indian government could reverse its opposition to the treaty without serious loss of diplomatic credibility. To do a volte-face after twenty-seven years of steadfast opposition would undermine the reliability of India as an international partner. It would also raise questions about Indian diplomatic fortitude. If India could finally be persuaded to turn, would it not become more prone to unequal agreements?

Abstaining: the Nonnuclear Option   31

Third, to join the NPT, it is claimed, would inflame domestic opinion and destroy any political entity that proposed accession. To accept unequal international agreements would be seen as a reversion to near-colonial political status. Public anger would topple any government that took a decision to join the NPT and might so enrage opinion as to lead a successor government to go nuclear in defiance.

This is a powerful case. Not surprisingly, few in India support signing the NPT. Almost, no one does so publicly. According to a U.S. Information Agency survey, 60 percent of urban Indian college graduates agreed that India should not sign the NPT.[16] However, each part of the anti-NPT case deserves response.

The NPT Reconsidered

The first response to the anti-NPT arguments is that while discriminatory agreements and institutions should indeed be avoided, India and other countries have entered into such agreements and joined such institutions when the advantages of doing so have outweighed the costs. Indian membership in the United Nations is a good instance of a cost/benefit calculus that has overridden the claims of universalism. The five permanent members of the United Nations Security Council (U.K., France, Russia, China, and the U.S.) have special rights and obligations, a condition that India accepted from the inception of the UN. It did so because, on balance, it was better to have than not to have a world body. New Delhi's present position is that these special rights and obligations should be extended to include India. It is not India's position to revoke them.[17]

The fact that the NPT is attractive to the vast majority of states should also give one pause. While it is widely accepted that the treaty is in a formal sense discriminatory, most states have nonetheless joined. If we discount the possibility that these countries are ethically blind or diplomatically naïve and craven, their accession must signify that for many countries the overall advantages of the treaty outweigh the disadvantages, including its discriminatory character.

A second response is that when the two major nuclear weapons states, the U.S. and Russia, are making substantial progress toward disarmament and when various "standouts" have joined the NPT, to reconsider treaty membership may be entirely credible diplomatically.

The destruction of U.S. and Russian tactical nuclear weapons and intermediate forces, and also the 50 percent cuts in strategic warheads, if carried through, will sharply reduce their inventories. Clearly, the two powers have at long last gone some way in meeting their NPT obligations. Of course, these reductions will leave enormous destructive power in American and Russian hands. Much more therefore needs to be done, but further deep cuts will be constrained by the kinds of technical and economic limits referred to earlier. Nevertheless, more cuts in nuclear weapons will likely be negotiated in the years to come. In addition, the decisions of China and France to join the NPT as nuclear weapons states, and South African accession to the treaty as a nonweapons state, have strengthened the agreement. Most recently, the U.S./North Korea deal has prevented a potentially serious defection from the treaty. Although the 1995 NPT Extension/Review Conference met few of the demands of the nonnuclear weapons states, the NPT structure is now more balanced and inclusive than ever before.

A third response is that public opposition to India joining the NPT is not some implacable, independent, and coherent force acting on government decision making. Indeed, the opposition to signing the NPT in India is not as pervasive or overwhelming as some assume. In the Kroc Institute survey, 39 percent of those polled support India acceding to the NPT either unilaterally or bilaterally with Pakistan. While the majority remains opposed to signing the NPT, conditions could change. Public opinion in India, as elsewhere, is in considerable part molded by political leadership and is therefore neither implacable nor independent. A stable leadership which outlined the advantages and disadvantages of joining the NPT and made a case for accession could change Indian opinion.

The larger point is that public opinion has undoubtedly constrained the Indian government's choices. There is very little informed understanding of the issues involved. It is suggested that this does not matter because the representatives of the Indian people, its Parliamentarians, have often indicated their overwhelming opposition to the NPT. So too have India's elites—in opinion surveys, in their writings, and in seminars. However, as Indian security analysts are painfully aware, while passions run high, sustained interest or expertise in defense matters, even among elite groups, runs low. This does not mean that Indian members of Parliament and the elite can be ignored; but to claim that their views are well-informed is to claim too much. India is hardly unique with respect to public apathy and ignorance on defense issues; but that is just the point.

In addition, the Kroc Institute poll suggests that, for the elite, the nuclear issue per se is not a terribly salient one compared with other social, political, and economic problems: only 6 percent of the elite sample rated the issue as very important. Communalism, poverty, economic stability, and terrorism rated much higher: between 30 and 52 percent of the respondents rated these issues as very important.

Ignorance of defense matters and the low salience of the nuclear issue together suggest that, if the Indian government were to make a strong case for reconsidering NPT membership, opposition would not necessarily be insurmountable. Moreover, the United States Information Agency and the Kroc Institute survey data suggest that if India were to take steps toward reducing tensions with Pakistan and strengthening global security regimes, support for India's participation in the NPT would grow.

Cutting a Regional Deal

Bilateral abstinence could also be concluded outside the NPT. It could be a strictly India/Pakistan regional agreement (e.g., a nuclear weapon–free zone). This is usually dismissed as "the NPT by another name," and the three criticisms against the NPT route apply here as well.

A regional agreement can also be criticized on the grounds that, while it may have the effect of the NPT in stopping additional proliferation, it does not offer the full range of treaty benefits. For instance, India within the NPT could be a greater force in modifying elements of the treaty and in persuading the nuclear weapons states to fulfill their two key obligations: reducing and eventually abolishing their arsenals and facilitating the peaceful uses of nuclear energy among the nonnuclear weapons signatories.

Perhaps the only conceivable advantage of an India/Pakistan agreement is that New Delhi could continue to claim that it had not retreated from its original opposition to the NPT. On balance, though, a regional agreement to abstain is probably inferior to signing the NPT.

Technical Limits to Unconditional Bilateralism

If most of the opposition to the NPT or the regional route to abstinence has so far been ethical, diplomatic, and political, it is now becoming increasingly technical. It is being argued that there is no technically foolproof method, unilateral or multilateral, of preventing and policing the illicit diversion of radioactive materials into nuclear weapons production. The examples of Iraq and North Korea lend credence to this argument. In spite of Iraqi and North Korean membership in the NPT, and in spite of IAEA certification suggesting compliance, both states violated the treaty. In the case of Iraq, despite military defeat and years of highly intrusive investigations by international inspectors, there remains a concern that the full extent of the program has not yet been unearthed and that not all of it has been eradicated.[18]

There is also growing concern that the NPT, regional agreements, and various supplemental measures are inadequate in preventing and policing the diversion of radioactive and weapons-grade materials from the former Soviet Union, materials which could find their way to Pakistan. These materials, plus the emigration of scientists from the former Soviet

Union in search of employment, could be used to produce nuclear weapons clandestinely.[19]

If a foolproof accounting of fissionable materials is beyond present capabilities, proliferation might yet be stopped or slowed by enacting a CTB. This supplement to the nonproliferation regime would help prevent the testing of weapons produced from illegally diverted materials. But Indian critics point out that the CTB route is also flawed. Computer-simulated testing and zero-yield tests are beyond the reach of a CTB and may be sufficiently reliable in certifying the efficacy of a weapons design. In sum, Pakistan could hide a nuclear weapons program from the NPT or from a regional mechanism and could unveil it at a time of its choosing to intimidate India.

While there is merit in these arguments, several replies may be essayed. First, Iraqi and North Korean violations did indeed escape the inspection regime, but surely it cannot be overlooked that both states were eventually caught. Moreover, whatever the legality and morality of the war against Iraq, it may have laid the basis for a more intrusive inspections regime. Again, while the recent U.S./North Korea nuclear deal has been criticized on various grounds, it is an indication that the nonproliferation effort should move in the direction of an "NPT plus" structure—constraints supplemented by incentives.

Second, the possibility of leaks from the former Soviet Union argues for greater, not less, multilateral regulation of nuclear programs. If the NPT did not exist, something like it would have to be invented.

Third, whereas the CTB is not a perfect solution in respect of testing, the best should not become the enemy of the good. Moreover, the reliability of computer-simulated and zero-yield laboratory tests is arguable. It is far from clear that the political leadership and also the armed forces of any state will gamble with weapons that have only been certified by quasi-testing. Perhaps such untested weapons might be used as a desperate last resort to stave off military defeat, or as retaliation against a nuclear strike, but they would be an unlikely choice for an aggressive first strike.

Last and most important, while the NPT, the complex of agreements relating to materials and personnel from former Soviet Union programs, and the CTB are individually flawed, together they help to strengthen the global nuclear nonproliferation regime. This enhanced regime, moreover, is consistent with the Indian goal of slowing or stopping Pakistani nuclearization. This is well enough understood in India. But it is India's calculation that the regime will or will not constrain Pakistan despite Indian participation in it. Thus, India could have a large slice of its nuclear cake and eat it too, by enjoying the benefits of the NPT without the burdens of joining it.

The China Syndrome

Whether bilateral abstinence is through the NPT or a regional mechanism, there remains the problem of China. In either case, India would be left without a deterrent against Chinese nuclear weapons.

It is argued that Chinese nuclear intimidation may occur in various circumstances. First, there remains the unresolved border dispute between the two countries. Second, internal instabilities in China could encourage external adventurousness. As the Chinese leadership struggles to assert or retain political control, it may be tempted to use external "threats" to outmaneuver and discipline internal rivals. Third, the two countries, by virtue of their size and self-image, are likely to be perennial rivals for influence in Asia if not farther afield.[20]

Nuclear asymmetry, it is thought, will strengthen Beijing's hand in each case. It will encourage obduracy over the border issue. Should instabilities in Tibet, and other areas of southern China, tempt the leadership to "teach" India a lesson (as a way of rallying support domestically), this temptation will be reinforced by nuclear superiority. And China's nuclear confidence will enable it to enlarge its spheres of influence to India's detriment.

Each of these propositions bears examination. First, while the border dispute is unresolved in a formal sense, Beijing has already obtained most of what it wanted out of the issue. If its primary aim was to secure the route from Xinkiang to Tibet, it long ago accomplished its goal. China is the satisfied power on the border issue, and it did not need nuclear weapons then, and does not need them now, to achieve its purpose.

Second, there is considerable room for debate over the internal/external linkage. Were internal factors truly responsible for Beijing's punitive wars against India and Vietnam? How vulnerable and unstable is China likely to be in the future? Can domestic political troubles be eased in the new China by external distractions? Last and most important, would war with India be credible, given that the only serious bilateral issue, namely the border, favors China; and would it help or hurt an insecure regime or leadership to raise an India bogey in such circumstances?

Third, the idea that nuclear weapons enhance China's status (and the status of the other nuclear weapons states) is a constant theme in Indian thinking, but there are reasons to be skeptical.[21] China's growing stature in recent decades is far more probably linked to quite different factors: the speed with which, after 1949, the new government asserted political control and embarked on social reforms; the dramatic improvements in the quality of physical life; the willingness to use force, as demonstrated by its interventions in Tibet and Korea in the 1950s and its defeat of India in 1962; the break with the Soviets in 1958; the increasing sophistication of its conventional forces over the past two decades; the dynamism of its economy over the past fifteen years; and, despite a certain measure of turbulence, overall political stability.

Nuclear weapons have not hurt China's standing in world affairs; but to ascribe the rise in Chinese status and influence primarily to nuclear weapons is untenable. The rise of both nonnuclear Germany and Japan as great powers, based on economic prowess, and the decay and collapse of a nuclear-ridden Soviet Union, further challenge the linkage between nuclear weapons, status, and influence. What is evident now is that a nuclear India would be unable to match China for status and influence unless it made important economic, social, and political changes. The real "race" with China is civic, not military.

In sum, then, the notion of a Chinese nuclear threat is questionable. If we add to this the progress made in India/China relations since 1988, then the likelihood of nuclear intimidation across the Himalayas seems even more remote. This is a judgment supported by the Kroc Institute poll, which reports that few see China as a factor in India's nuclear choices. Only 17 percent of those who support keeping the option open wanted India to go nuclear in case of a serious deterioration in relations with China. On the other hand, 52 percent and 48 percent respectively supported going nuclear in response to threats from other nuclear powers or a Pakistani nuclear test. Among the nuclear advocates, only 20 percent perceived a major threat from China, while 57 percent cited threats from nuclear Pakistan. The China factor is not a major consideration in public thinking about nuclear policy options for India. Contrary to official policy in New Delhi, which places major emphasis on the potential threat from China, the public does not currently perceive major danger in relations with Beijing.

Unconditional Abstinence and Nuclear Asymmetry

The case against unconditional unilateral abstinence rests primarily on the military consequences of nuclear asymmetry in an India/China or an India/Pakistan confrontation. As suggested earlier, an India/China confrontation leading to Chinese nuclear threats seems improbable. What then might be the military consequence of asymmetry in an India/Pakistan confrontation?

Nuclear Asymmetry and its Consequences

The most likely battleground between India and Pakistan will be Kashmir. In a situation of asymmetry, a nuclear-armed Pakistan could be encouraged to launch a conventional attack against Indian Kashmir. Without nuclear weapons of its own or a nuclear umbrella from a weapons power, India would have two responses: to counterattack elsewhere along the front, and to fight in Kashmir. However, both options would be untenable. A counterattack in Punjab and Sindh, to relieve pressure along the northern axis, would be deterred by the threat of Pakistani counterforce and countervalue nuclear strikes, that is, by attacks on military and civilian targets, respectively.

If India decided not to counterattack in Punjab and Sindh but chose instead to stop and then repel the invasion of Kashmir, any concentration of Indian forces for defense would be deterred by the threat of nuclear attack, either on its forces or on value targets outside Kashmir (not in Kashmir, because to do so is to destroy the prize itself). In addition, Pakistan could threaten to use nuclear weapons on vital supply routes such as the Banihal Tunnel, thus isolating Indian forces in Kashmir and preventing their resupply.

Conscious of these possibilities arising from nuclear asymmetry, India would be deterred from mounting a defense. If it was not deterred, then it would be severely punished by the use of nuclear weapons against military and civilian targets, at which point any further defense would collapse. Military initiative, concentration of military force, and military superiority, three key ingredients of success, would reside with Pakistan.[22]

A second possibility in Kashmir is that Pakistan would escalate its support to the insurgents. The pressure in India to respond more forcefully to the militants would grow. As the Indian army increased the scope and intensity of operations, a nuclear Pakistan could issue a warning that any escalation within Indian Kashmir would be punished by nuclear attack. This might include demonstration strikes, with the threat of counterforce and countervalue strikes to follow if New Delhi refused to stand down. Without nuclear weapons, it might be argued, India would be deterred from enlarging its counterinsurgency campaign.

Nuclear Asymmetry Revisited

While neither case can be dismissed lightly, at least four counterarguments may be advanced. None of these replies is necessarily decisive, but together they increase confidence in the plausibility of unconditional unilateralism.

The first counterargument maintains that Pakistan will find it morally and diplomatically difficult to use nuclear weapons in this way, particularly if India's response is simply to defend in Kashmir. Nuclear threats and nuclear attack against a nuclear-free opponent are obviously not unprecedented; but for over fifty years neither have they been morally and diplomatically unencumbered.

The U.S. and the Soviet Union have made nuclear threats on several occasions since 1945; and the U.S. carried out the one and only nuclear attack.[23] The U.S. continues to reserve the right to use both threats and attack against nonnuclear foes. However, there remains controversy over the efficacy of nuclear threats. In one of the most significant incidents, Richard Nixon's "madman" threat to Ho Chi Minh in the fall of 1969, the gambit utterly failed to force Vietnamese concessions.[24] The credibility of such threats is often doubtful, especially in relation to crises that do not pose a strategic danger to the nation issuing the threats. Moreover, the widespread public revulsion that would likely result from the first use of nuclear weapons serves as a major political deterrent to carrying out such threats. As a measure of this international distaste for nuclear weapons, it is instructive that neither the U.S. nor the Soviets have overtly publicized or celebrated the occasions on which they have had to threaten nuclear use. This reflects, on the one hand, a realpolitik appreciation that to do so would encourage others to go nuclear; and, on the other hand, an unwillingness to admit to nuclear bullying.

As to nuclear attack, the use of nuclear weapons in 1945 occurred in very special circumstances, circumstances that are unlikely to be repeated in an India/Pakistan, and specifically Kashmir, context. For one thing, Japan was the original aggressor in the war against China and then the U.S. and its allies, and was morally vulnerable as a result. For another, the Japanese were the objects of widespread international opprobrium, not only for their original sin but for the brutality of their occupation and conduct of war. Lastly, dropping the bomb on Hiroshima and Nagasaki was unconstrained at the time by any immediate mobilization of public revulsion against the use of nuclear weapons.

India must of course expect that Pakistan will attempt to paint it the original aggressor in Kashmir. Moreover, human rights failures and the travails of democracy in Kashmir may continue to keep New Delhi on the defensive internationally. However, there is little prospect that India's record on Kashmir will be so egregious as to cause widespread agreement on New Delhi's exclusive guilt in fueling tensions and on the justice of nuclear punishment. More telling perhaps, five decades after the bombing of Hiroshima and Nagasaki there is a very substantial amount of international public opinion against nuclear threats and nuclear punishment, opinion which could be mobilized to hurt Pakistani interests more substantially than any possible gain in Kashmir.

International opinion is moved not just by a moral revulsion against nuclear weapons but also by diplomatic prudence. It is diplomatic prudence to fear the naturalizing of nuclear weapons as "just another weapon." To stand idle as the taboo against nuclear threats and punishment is violated is to increase the likelihood of nuclear intimidation and attack by other powers in other places. In addition, actual nuclear use in an India/Pakistan situation may be directly consequential for others. For instance, the spread of radioactive fallout is not just an internal, bilateral, or even regional problem, but potentially a transregional, even global one. The environmental sensitivity of publics, and therefore of governments vis-à-vis the actions of other governments, should not be underestimated and will only heighten in the years to come.

A second counterargument relates to the role of the nuclear powers, particularly the U.S. and Russia. It has been argued that it is unlikely that the nuclear powers will intervene against Pakistan in a crisis. This may turn out to be the case of course. But it is worth pausing over why they may have to intervene. Any nuclear-armed great power which turns a blind eye to the use of nuclear threats by lesser powers must reckon that it "would have little standing as a global power in South Asia or elsewhere if it permitted Pakistan to practice nuclear intimidation with impunity."[25]

The third and more telling counterargument is that, confronted by an India which has unconditionally and verifiably renounced nuclear weapons, Pakistan will find it extremely difficult to keep its nuclear option open, to go nuclear outright, or to remain nuclear. International opinion and pressures will be exerted against Islamabad as never before. Though Pakistan can attempt to deflect international opinion and pressures by claiming that only nuclear weapons can counter India's more or less permanent superiority in conventional forces and strategic depth, this can be expected to encounter considerable opposition.

It will be argued against Islamabad that Pakistani deficiencies and fears are correctable, in at least two ways. First, Pakistan can be promised enough additional conventional arms to enable it to deter India and to defend itself should deterrence break down. Second, instead of "leveling up" the quantum of conventional forces, it is possible to "level down" so that both sides have enough defense against each other, as well as third parties and internal enemies. With its dramatic nuclear gesture, India will have opened the door to negotiating a conventional force balance which is consonant with Pakistani security needs. The Conventional Forces in Europe (CFE) agreement, signed after the Intermediate Nuclear Forces treaty (INF), shows that this can be achieved. A South Asian balance will not be easy to construct, given that both sides have to maintain forces for other opponents and for internal security; but negotiated sufficiency and a nonprovocative defense are not impossible either.[26]

Of the two correctives, leveling down is preferable. One advantage of going nuclear, it is usually argued, is that it saves expenditure on expensive conventional arms. Therefore, Pakistan can object that it is cheaper to match India's conventional superiority with nuclear capability than with increased conventional capability. Leveling down to a conventional balance that satisfies both sides and avoids a costly arms race can overcome this objection. Level-down negotiations would focus on reducing inventories of offensive weapon systems on both sides, that is, systems which encourage thoughts of a first strike and tend to be more expensive. The question of what constitutes an offensive weapon and what is a defensive weapon is a difficult one. All weapons can be used for offensive purposes. However, it is at least possible to agree on which systems are *more* and which are *less* offensive weapons and what should be the appropriate mix of these.[27]

A final counterargument is military. It is said that only nuclear weapons can deter nuclear weapons.[28] Only when a nuclear threat can be matched by a nuclear counterthreat and when a nuclear strike promises to be matched by a nuclear counterstrike can stability be achieved. Thus, if India is to deter a nuclear-armed Pakistan, it must be armed with nuclear weapons as weapons of retaliation. While this is a classic formulation, it bears some reexamination.

It is at least conceivable that the threat of a nuclear attack can be matched by the threat of massive conventional retaliation.[29] India could threaten to retaliate with massive conventional bombing of Pakistani population centers, industrial sites, infrastructure, nuclear facilities, and symbolic targets. Indian bombers and missiles, armed with a variety of explosives and especially high-incendiary weapons, could credibly threaten enormous punitive raids. Cities, major industrial sites, chemical factories, nuclear reactors, dams, irrigation canals, and hydropower works all could be targeted for conventional attack.[30] Important symbolic targets, particularly major places of worship, would also be priorities. In short, it is possible to envisage a conventional force structure, married to an appropriate doctrine, which could mimic or near-mimic the indiscriminate damage that nuclear strikes would inflict. The point is not to advocate such a scenario but to illustrate that modern conventional weapons are so destructive that they can nearly match the devastation that would be caused by a nuclear attack. If deterrence of threatened nuclear aggression is the goal, it can be accomplished through conventional means.

That said, it is true that Pakistan would achieve at least as much, if not absolutely more damage with nuclear strikes; but a strategy of massive conventional retaliation would mean that Pakistan would be horribly maimed as well.[31] Indeed, in relative terms it might even be worse off, given that India has a population and land area that is roughly eight times the size of Pakistan's.

Implementing a conventional retaliatory strategy of any seriousness would encounter three limits or objections. First, if Pakistan's nuclear arsenal was large enough, then India's most important air and missile in-

Abstaining: the Nonnuclear Option 41

stallations would be vulnerable to a first strike, and massive conventional retaliation would become impossible. Secondly, a strategy of massive conventional retaliation would be expensive. India would need to mount enormous raids capable of getting past Pakistani air defenses. This would require considerable superiority in aircraft and missiles and enormous stocks of conventional explosives. The cost of these, and the investments in skilled labor, would add to India's defense bill. However, these added costs would need to be balanced against the costs of nuclear weapons which, if properly computed, are hardly modest. Moreover, since nuclear weapons are not necessarily substitutable for conventional weapons, a nuclear deterrent would entail large and expensive conventional forces as well.[32] Finally, a strategy of massive conventional retaliation is open to the charge that, if it mimics nuclear retaliation, it might as well be nuclear. This is correct. But the obverse is also correct. Neither side needs to go nuclear to achieve mutual terror and mutual deterrence, if that is the objective.

Nuclear Abstinence: Viable and Advisable?

A policy option is credible if it is not only strategically viable but also strategically advisable and if, in addition, it is politically feasible. Abstinence is viable; but is it advisable?

Viability

Strategic viability refers here to the practicability of a course of action, and it rests on two tests: Is it plausible in light of India's security concerns (where security has a broader connotation than merely military); and is it internationally acceptable?

If this dual test is applied, it would appear that the two conditional options are the least-viable forms of abstinence. Nuclear guarantees are no longer plausible in Indian security thinking. In addition, they are unlikely to be offered by the nuclear powers. Phased disarmament is congenial to India but will not be acceptable to the nuclear powers. Of the two unconditional options, unilateral rather than bilateral abstinence seems the more viable. A unilateral decision to renounce nuclear weapons with no conditions attached could be consonant with Indian security: there is a high probability that it will cause Islamabad to follow suit, and if not, India could be made secure by a strategy of massive conventional retaliation. Furthermore, it will require no international negotiations—not with Pakistan, the NPT signatories, or the other nuclear powers—and will therefore have the advantage of easy international acceptability. The unilateral approach is not very popular, however. Among nuclear opponents in the Kroc Institute poll, only 17 percent favored unilateral renunciation.

Advisability

Nuclear abstinence must not only be viable but also positively advisable in strategic terms. That is, in the end, those who advocate it must satisfactorily answer the following difficult question: Why change course? Why not keep the nuclear option open? A thoroughgoing answer is beyond the scope of the present essay. However, the following is a prolegomenon to an answer.

First, over time, keeping the option open is not likely to be credible to the other nuclear powers and may therefore seriously complicate India's strategic environment. The "neither-confirm-nor-deny" posture of half-truths, hints, calculated leaks, and genuine revelations will cumulate at some point to persuade outsiders that India is virtually a nuclear power, perhaps armed with an arsenal of "short-order" weapons (that is, weapons that could be assembled and fired at short notice) and possessing missiles capable of striking well beyond the region or near-region.[33] Indeed most analysts in the West assume that India is in fact a nuclear power with an arsenal of already assembled or "short-order" weapons that could be pressed into action in a military emergency. Because of this perception, India's declarations for nuclear disarmament are not taken seriously by some, and its aspirations for global leadership have been frustrated.

The current posture of nuclear ambiguity has created a "lose/lose" situation: India is considered a de facto nuclear power, and as such is subject to intense nonproliferation pressures from the major powers. There is even the possibility that the nuclear powers might target India with their weapons. As the impression grows that India is a virtual nuclear power, it could become a target as part of general deterrence policy. This would very likely be the case with China (which is rumored to have missiles in Tibet, pointed at India), but also perhaps with the U.S. and Russia. Nuclear ambiguity may deter an equally ambiguous Pakistan, but it may expose India to several further layers of nuclear threat, thereby greatly increasing its strategic risk: Nothing fails like success.

Ambiguity also exposes India to political and economic threats. To persuade the Indian government to give up the ambiguity posture, the nuclear powers could exploit India's internal political problems, particularly its ethnic and religious divisions. Kashmir, in this regard, becomes distinctly vulnerable. Other punishments might include economic sanctions and technology denials. Indeed the United States has already exerted pressures on several occasions to block transactions perceived as violating nonproliferation norms, most prominently in the purchase of cryogenic rocket components from Russia.

Second, while nuclear ambiguity may be "deterrence-stable," it may not be "crisis-stable," and therefore it is not a tenable position in the end.

Whereas uncertainty of nuclear retaliation may deter potential adversaries in the general course of things, in a crisis, which is an environment marked by the dangerous lack of certitudes and by shortened decision-making horizons, what is likely to be stabilizing is certainty of response. If one side or the other calculates that the other side's ambiguity is too ambiguous, it might decide to strike first. At a critical moment, ambiguity may give its possessor a false sense of security and its opponent a false sense of opportunity. This is why India's present position is not a stable one and why it will move gradually in the direction of an overt posture. Those who support ambiguity must therefore live with the strong possibility that the nuclear advocates are likely to win the day against the supporters of official policy.

Third, the supporters of official policy cannot draw comfort from the fact that the decay of ambiguity into weaponization will be in the direction of more or less permanent stability, as argued by the proponents of going nuclear. Those who argue for an overt posture—whether fully weaponized or short-order weaponized—argue that, once both sides go openly nuclear, mutual deterrence will be possible and that this will stabilize the military relationship. The problem is that this gives every conflict, of which there are many, the possibility of escalating to nuclear confrontation. The stability of nuclear deterrence that strategists often extol is a terrifying phenomenon, one in which military or political disputes can lead rapidly to the brink of Armageddon. U.S. and Soviet officials came perilously close to this precipice during the 1962 Cuban Missile Crisis and on several other occasions during the cold war. If overt nuclear deterrence were to come to South Asia, the India/Pakistan conflict, especially Kashmir, could become the basis for nuclear confrontation.

There is a fatal flaw in deterrence, and it is not simply the flaw that nuclear advocates recognize, namely, that if something can go wrong it will go wrong. The deeper argument is that something will inevitably go wrong: deterrence will undo deterrence. The argument depends on the proposition that if deterrence is built on the certainty of retaliatory punishment in the face of an attack, then over time it must be prone to decay. This is because the only way to be relatively sure that someone will carry out a threat is if they carry it out from time to time. With nuclear weapons this is not possible. Thus, the certainty of retaliation can only be approached asymptotically. To communicate certainty of response needs ever greater investments in military capabilities, or it needs ever more credible demonstrations of commitment, or both. The problem is that as capabilities and shows of commitment inflate, the opponent will have difficulty in distinguishing between a deterrence posture and a first-strike posture. When that time comes, the incentive for the opponent to go first will be high. Moreover, the deterrer, recognizing this incentive, will contemplate preempting preemption. And the opponent, recognizing the deterrer's incentive to preempt preemption, will be tempted to preempt the deterrer's preemptive preemption. And so on, in an infinite regress, till deterrence blows up. This is the theoretic basis for the view that deterrence is ultimately unstable and that disarmament or abstinence is imperative.[34]

In addition, there are more "idiosyncratic" limits to nuclear deterrence in South Asia. The region cannot draw easy sustenance from the experience of the U.S. and former Soviet Union. Geographically, the two superpowers were not contiguous and were not therefore prone to everyday frictions. Historically, they developed largely in isolation from each other. What is more important is that they had never fought one another, and neither side harbored territorial claims against the other. After 1945, while the two were engaged in a geopolitical and ideological contest of great seriousness, at the people-to-people level there was little real animosity. Militarily, from 1941 to 1945, they were allies against fascist Germany, and therefore after the Second World War they had a history of military cooperation and military respect which helped stabilize their cold war rivalry. In addition, geographic distance helped militarily, especially in the early years when the nuclear relationship was in its infancy and its dynamics in flux. Without missiles in their armories, strategic warning time, that is, the time from the launch of an aircraft to its arrival over the other's territory, was greater.[35]

India and Pakistan do not have these ameliorating conditions. Geographically, they are contiguous over a long border, a border which is bitterly contested by at least one side and is prone to everyday frictions. Historically, their development as nation-states has been ineluctably intertwined. Moreover, their history is as much a history of war as of peace, and they continue to quarrel over territory, preeminently Kashmir. Their rivalry is not just over territory and ideology, but is marked in addition by suspicion at a people-to-people level. They have never been military allies, and, while their armed forces share a great deal, there is a fair degree of mutual contempt. Finally, strategic warning times in South Asia, even with aircraft, are measured in minutes and with missiles will be even less.

This does not mean that India and Pakistan cannot evolve some form of deterrence, but it does mean that deterrence in South Asia will have its own special problems and they may be far more difficult ones than in the case of the U.S. and Soviet Union.

Fourth, if ambiguity is sought for deterrence, it is worth recalling what can be deterred and what cannot be deterred. Some have argued that ambiguity generates a form of "existential" deterrence, that the uncertainty of possession of nuclear weapons is sufficient for deterrence in South

Asia. It was suggested earlier that while this may be so, crisis stability may not be ensured by such a posture. But a more fundamental point is: what can nuclear deterrence deter?

It bears repeating that it cannot deter perhaps the most important sources of violence in the region, namely, insurgency and terrorism. Indeed, in a perverse way, it may make the region more hospitable to both. With India and Pakistan at par in their ambiguous nuclear postures, Islamabad is free to export violence.[36] On the other hand, if both sides abjured nuclear weapons, Pakistani intervention would be exceedingly dangerous. Abstinent Pakistan would have to reckon that abstinent India might retaliate by "hot-pursuit" strikes, with the promise of escalation to outright conventional war. However, a strategy of conventional escalation, beyond some minimal level, becomes impossible when nuclear weapons are or may be available to the enemy.[37] In sum, nuclear weapons, declared or undeclared, have made low-intensity subversion more likely than before. Abstinence would at least return the military initiative to India and in doing so might staunch the flow of external aid to subversion.

Fifth, keeping the option open as part, or all, of a deterrence posture contributes to the freezing of India/Pakistan relations. It postpones the day when the two sides must confront the fundamental causes of their quarrels and how those quarrels can be resolved short of war. And it will entrench those on both sides who have an interest in permanent enmity, thereby prolonging the region's state of war. In sum, the stability of deterrence is the stability of a cold and negative peace.

Lastly, keeping the option open will continue to adversely affect India's domestic politics and the welfare of its citizens. A "neither-confirm-nor-deny" policy—unlike abstinence or even weaponization—must perforce be built on secrecy and obfuscation, to the detriment of a tradition of public accountability indispensable in a democracy. In addition, such a policy will be to the long-term detriment of Indian science, of the nuclear program itself, and to the health of the Indian people.

India's nuclear program is not the only area prone to secrecy and obfuscation, but its "success" in avoiding the public gaze will contribute to a political culture of lies and evasions, which in the long term will degrade Indian democracy. This culture of lies and evasions must harm the larger enterprise of Indian science and technology. If one of the largest and most prestigious areas of scientific and technological endeavor becomes prone to such a culture, it is hard to see how other areas can escape the miasma. Then there are the costs to the program itself. The most extraordinary legislation has been passed to "protect" the Indian nuclear program from public scrutiny.[38] This risks undermining public support for the nuclear program. A program regulated primarily by internal scrutiny will be inefficient and dangerous, and, if and when its wastefulness and harmfulness become apparent, public reaction may be to terminate the program altogether.[39] Lastly, nuclear technology is not a forgiving technology. A shrouded program, not open to external criticism and regulation, is liable to malpractice and mismanagement, the effects of which could seriously jeopardize the health and safety of scores of citizens for a long time to come.[40]

Is Abstinence Feasible?

If abstinence is viable and advisable, is it politically feasible? It is an option that will obviously garner international and regional support, but equally will face stiff opposition within India. With only 8 percent support in the Kroc Institute survey, the proposals outlined here—renouncing the nuclear option either unilaterally or bilaterally—clearly lack substantial political backing. Nonetheless, the feasibility of nuclear abstinence could grow if it were backed by a political coalition formed to legitimize the concept and educate public opinion.

What kind of coalition will be needed? An effective coalition for change must consist of a strong and stable political leadership, one or more major political parties, an influential section of the press, an intellectual class or group, and elements of civil society, particularly pressure or interest groups operating in the issue area.

It will take a strong and stable leadership to articulate the costs and benefits of the move from ambiguity to abstinence and to publicize the calculus widely. As things stand, there is little prospect of strong and stable government in New Delhi. Most commentators predict that the present and foreseeable future of Indian electoral politics is one of short-lived minority and coalition governments. In any case, a government committed to abstinence must see nuclear politics as an important issue and must give it systematic policy attention. However, other problems are likely to rank higher in governmental priorities in coming years: economic reform; caste, ethnic, and religious quarrels; and a growing sense of public impatience with maladministration. Commerce, communalism, and corruption, not conquest, will continue to dominate the political agenda.

The lack of policy attention to nuclear issues might be compensated, to some extent, by a specialized agency made responsible for systematically analyzing and articulating the costs of various nuclear choices. Neither the Ministry of Defence nor the Ministry of External Affairs is equipped to carry out such a task. A National Security Council (NSC), long debated in India, appears to be in the offing, but it is unlikely to be given the responsibility or bureaucratic capacity to deal with such questions of fundamental policy choice.

Abstaining: the Nonnuclear Option 47

Even if the highest political leadership of the country was interested in reviewing India's nuclear choices, it would need the support of one or more of the major political parties. Currently, no party is inclined toward change in India's nuclear posture. A major obstacle to change is that the rank and file of most parties pays very little attention to military and diplomatic issues; they have been kept ill-informed by governments that have had no desire to share information on nuclear matters; and they possess little capacity to form independent judgments on the strategic pluses and minuses of various options. The party that pays the greatest attention to nuclear issues and that has acquired some knowledge on the question is the Bharatiya Janata Party (BJP), but it is the most supportive of outright nuclearization and the least inclined to give up the option.

A review of nuclear attitudes and policies will also require the participation and cooperation of the press. In an open society such as India, the press performs two functions: it disseminates policy-relevant information to the public, and it helps guard the public interest by assessing the correctness of government policies. Any Indian government interested in a review of nuclear policy would have to enlist the print and broadcast media in the task of distributing information vital to an informed public debate. It must also persuade respected commentators that a reassessment of nuclear policy is necessary.

The Indian press is central to the prospects of policy change. It gives more attention to nuclear issues than perhaps any other institution in public life. Indeed, judging by coverage in the powerful English press, one would imagine that India's nuclear choices are the most important issues facing the nation. The press also has a certain amount of expertise. It has an outreach unrivaled by any other institution except the government itself. Most important, though, it is a sector of society that governments seem to fear. While political leaders can and often do manipulate and even coerce the fourth estate, the press remains a formidable institution. The strength and relative independence of the press make it the key actor, apart from the government itself, in any crusade for abstinence. Thus far the press has either been supportive of the government's ambiguity policy or it has urged outright nuclearization. Any Indian government interested in the abstinence option would therefore have to convert the press: the Indian press will not, of its own accord, lead any kind of charge for abstinence.

A powerful and strongly motivated intellectual community can make a difference in the nuclear debate. Academics, think-tank analysts, and other commentators often function to legitimize policy. They possess the power, beyond any simple reckoning of their numbers, to propose and oppose changes. Unfortunately, there are few academics trained in strategic studies, and even less are willing to challenge the prevailing nuclear policy. Indian think tanks are also few, and almost none have the inclination or capacity to get involved in nuclear matters. The weakness of the community is in large part due to the Indian government's reluctance to encourage the conduct of open, free, and comprehensive debate on nuclear issues. Indian academics, for the most part, are paid and funded by the government. Think tanks are still dependent on government goodwill for their existence and functioning. Not surprisingly, recent debates within the scholarly community have been confined to how India should respond to U.S. nonproliferation pressures and to technical issues raised by a comprehensive test ban or fissile material cutoff. Intellectuals have steered clear of more thoroughgoing assessments of the nuclear issue.

Finally, a nuclear review and the abstinence option could be urged and supported by nongovernmental organizations (NGOs). Presently, however, there are no major NGOs focused on nuclear policy. Some environmental and women's groups are concerned about the impact of certain government programs and conceptions of national security, but these organizations are not focused on the nuclear issue per se. They see nuclear programs and the prospect of nuclear weapons as an instance of the kind of government policy they oppose and as incorporating a conception of security that is inimical to their values. However, nuclear policy is not the specific concern that spurs their activities. Beyond this, there is no major antinuclear movement in India, except for some localized opposition to nuclear plants which, because of the threat of radiation, are perceived as a public hazard. Given these limitations, a serious and sustained NGO intervention in the nuclear weapons debate seems unlikely.

Does this mean that a "winning" coalition for abstinence is impossible, that there is no hope for nuclear renunciation? Three years ago many analysts would have dismissed the possibility of economic reforms in India as equally unlikely. A relatively weak coalition government nevertheless managed to institute dramatic economic change. Is something equally unforeseen possible in the area of nuclear policy? Probably not, but conditions could change rapidly if a crisis was brought on by external pressure and/or internal demands for change. Crises, by definition, are unpredictable. In the wake of the NPT's extension, one can almost certainly predict that external pressures on India to give up the weapon option will increase. The more decisive possibility would be an internal push for change. This seems unlikely now, but developments within the nuclear program itself could alter this circumstance. If India's nuclear program, opaque as it is, was to show signs of increasing technical, safety, and financial difficulty, public support might quickly erode.

Is abstinence viable? Probably so. Is it strategically advisable? For various reasons, especially in the long run, yes. Is it politically feasible? Here the answer is more uncertain. The case in favor of renouncing the nuclear

Abstaining: the Nonnuclear Option 49

option is compelling. This essay has argued it on moral, political, military, security, economic, and environmental grounds. Whether the requisite political leadership will rise to take up this case remains to be seen. The traditions of India's founders, especially the principles of nonviolence espoused by Gandhi and Nehru, would seem to fit well with a politics of nuclear abstinence, but such ideas are out of favor in today's India. The contemporary emphasis is on national strength, communal pride, and economic growth. It will take renewed commitment to the Gandhian vision and an ability to see beyond current conditions to create a political climate conducive to nuclear abstinence.

Notes

1. Ziba Moshaver, *Nuclear Weapons Proliferation in the Indian Subcontinent* (New York: St. Martin's Press, 1991), 35.

2. Shyam Bhatia, *India's Nuclear Bomb* (New Delhi: Vikas, 1979), 116–17.

3. G.G. Mirchandani, *India's Nuclear Dilemma* (New Delhi: Popular Book Services, 1968), 54–56 and 99–100; Bhatia, *India's Nuclear Bomb*, 116–17.

4. See Dhirendra Sharma, *India's Nuclear Estate* (New Delhi: Lancers, 1983), 139–43 for some figures on how much was spent on the nuclear program relative to other science and technology sectors in the period 1974–83.

5. For evidence of dissent within the nuclear establishment on the workings of the program, see Dhirendra Sharma, *The Indian Atom: Power and Proliferation* (New Delhi: Philosophy and Social Action, 1986), 92–95.

6. I base these observations on my personal contact with certain environmental and women's groups in and around Baroda in Gujarat in 1990–91.

7. See Amitabh Mattoo, "The Campaign for Nuclear Disarmament: A Study of its Re-emergence, Growth and Decline in the 1980s" (D. Phil. diss., Faculty of Social Studies, University of Oxford, 1992).

8. "Mistakenly" because there may be no field left. Even a limited nuclear exchange, as suggested by the nuclear winter hypothesis, could be catastrophic globally. See Carl Sagan, *A Path Where No Man Thought: Nuclear Winter and the End of the Arms Race* (New York: Random House, 1990).

9. Pran Chopra, "For a World Freed of the Nuclear Menace," in *The Diffusion of Advanced Weaponry: Technologies, Regional Implications, and Responses*, eds. W. Thomas Wander, Eric H. Arnett, and Paul Bracken (Washington, D.C.: American Association for the Advancement of Science, 1994), 356–62.

10. Richard Garwin, "Nuclear Weapons for the United Nations," in *A Nuclear-Weapon-Free-World: Desirable, Feasible?* eds. Joseph Rotblat, et al. (Boulder, Colo.: Westview, 1993), 169–80.

11. Francesco Calogero, "An Asymptotic Approach to a NWFW," in *A Nuclear-Weapon-Free-World: Desirable, Feasible?* eds. Joseph Rotblat, et al. (Boulder, Colo.: Westview, 1993), 191–200.

12. Reference here is to the "Action Plan for a Nuclear-Weapons Free and Non-Violent World Order" submitted to the United Nations Third Special Session on Disarmament in New York, 9 June 1988. The plan has been updated to reflect changes since the end of the cold war. See the "Declaration Launching the Rajiv

Gandhi Memorial Initiative for the Advancement of Human Civilization," Rajiv Gandhi Foundation, New Delhi, 2 May 1993.

13. It is not clear which side is more to blame. The former Soviet Union, and then Russia, under Mikhail Gorbachev and Boris Yeltsin have generally seemed more willing to draw down their nuclear arsenals. On the other hand, the U.S. Department of Defense's recent "bottom up" review of U.S. nuclear posture suggests that American decision makers would go faster in disarming but for their judgement that the Russians and various "rogue" states remain possible nuclear threats.

14. The costs of denuclearization are dealt with in the contributions of Alexander G. Savelyev, Robert B. Barker, and Dipankar Bannerjee in *Weapons of Mass Destruction: Costs and Benefits*, ed. Kathleen Bailey (New Delhi: Manohar, 1994). Barker notes that the cleanup of U.S. facilities which contributed to nuclear weapons production will cost between $200,000 million and $1,000,000 million, that is, one trillion. In 1993, the U.S. Department of Energy spent over $5,000 million on environmental restoration and waste management. Barker concludes that at this rate it will take the U.S. 200 years to finish the cleanup! See Barker, "The Environmental Costs of the United States Nuclear Weapons Programme," 123.

15. On Chinese willingness to work for a CTB by 1996, see Dingli Shen, "The Prospects for a Comprehensive Test Ban Treaty: Implications of Chinese Nuclear Testing," in *Diffusion of Advanced Weaponry*, eds. Wander, Arnett, and Bracken, 280.

16. Elaine El Assal, "Most Urban Indians Still Oppose NPT," M-20-95, United States Information Agency *Opinion Analysis*, 27 January 1995, 5.

17. This is a point made also by Pran Chopra in his *India, Pakistan, and the Kashmir Tangle* (New Delhi: Indus, 1994), 49: ". . . India itself discriminates in applying that criterion [non-discrimination]: it is happy to be a member of the UN system in which some countries have the veto power and some not, and India would be still happier if it also acquired this discriminatory status."

18. P.R. Chari, "Indian Defence and Security: A Cost-Benefit Analysis of Nuclear Proliferation," in *Weapons of Mass Destruction*, ed. Bailey, 97–99. Chari refers to the Iraqi and North Korean case in the context of the "fragility of the non-proliferation regime."

19. Ibid., 98.

20. Some of these concerns are expressed by K. Subrahmanyam, "Implications of Nuclear Asymmetry," in *Nuclear Myths and Realities*, ed. K. Subrahmanyam (New Delhi: ABC Publishing House, 1981), 214–15.

21. See Subrahmanyam, "India's Dilemma," in *Nuclear Myths and Realities*, ed. Subrahmanyam, vii.

22. For an analysis of nuclear asymmetry roughly along these lines, see Subrahmanyam, "Implications of Nuclear Asymmetry," 201–209 and K. Sundarji, *Blind Men of Hindoostan: Indo-Pak Nuclear War* (New Delhi: UBS Publishers, 1993), 21–48.

23. For an examination of the U.S. use of nuclear threats see Daniel Ellsberg, "Introduction: A Call to Mutiny," in *Protest and Survive*, eds. E.P. Thompson and Dan Smith (New York: Monthly Review Press, 1981); see also Joseph Gerson, *With Hiroshima Eyes: Atomic War, Nuclear Extortion, and Moral Imagination* (Philadel-

phia: New Society Publishers, 1995).

24. The incident is described in Ellsberg, "Introduction: A Call to Mutiny," and in Richard Nixon, *RN: The Memoirs of Richard Nixon* (New York: Grosset and Dunlap, 1978), 393–405.

25. Sumit Ganguly, "Nuclear Issues in South Asia," in *The Diffusion of Advanced Weaponry*, eds. Wander, Arnett, and Bracken, 219.

26. The notion of defensive sufficiency occupies a prominent part in the recent attempts to delineate "cooperative security." See Janne Nolan, ed., *Global Engagement: Cooperation and Security in the 21st Century* (Washington, D.C.: The Brookings Institution, 1994). On applications to South Asia, see Kanti Bajpai and Stephen P. Cohen, "Cooperative Security and South Asian Insecurity," in *Global Engagement*, ed. Nolan, 447-80. On the notion of nonprovocative defense, see Bjorn Moeller, *Common Security and Non-Offensive Defense: A Neorealist Perspective* (Boulder: Lynne Rienner, 1992), and David Gates, *Non-Offensive Defence: An Alternative Strategy for NATO?* (London: St. Martin's Press, 1991).

27. For this argument, see Kanti Bajpai and Varun Sahni, *Secure and Solvent: Thinking About an Affordable Defense for India*, RGICS Paper No. 11, Rajiv Gandhi Institute for Contemporary Studies, New Delhi, May 1994, 28–31.

28. See Subrahmanyam, "Implications of Nuclear Asymmetry," in *Nuclear Myths and Realities*, ed. Subrahmanyam, 209: "Nuclear weapons can be deterred only by nuclear weapons."

29. K. Subrahmanyam in his writings has often drawn attention to the devastation of modern conventional warfare and how both the Eastern and Western blocs, conscious of this, chose to fight their mutual battles on Third World battlefields. The development of the air/land battle doctrine shows how shatteringly destructive a conventional response could be. The U.S.'s air attacks on Iraq are instructive in this regard.

30. On the strategic "uses" of enemy nuclear power plants, see Bennett Ramberg, *Nuclear Power Plants as Weapons for the Enemy: An Unrecognized Military Peril* (Berkeley, Calif.: Univ. of California Press, 1980).

31. Rashid Naim has calculated the kind of damage that might occur in an India/Pakistan nuclear war. See his "After Midnight," in *Nuclear Proliferation in South Asia*, ed. Stephen P. Cohen (Boulder, Colo.: Westview, 1991), 23–61.

32. On the broader costs of nuclear weapons, see the various essays in Bailey, ed., *Weapons of Mass Destruction*.

33. See the view expressed in "Bundy, Crowe, and Drell—A Program for Reducing the Nuclear Danger: But No Short Road to Disarmament" in the *Carnegie Quarterly* 38, nos. 3, 4 (Summer/Fall 1993): 5–6: "As to the unannounced nuclear-weapons states—Israel, India, and Pakistan—the cochairmen [i.e., McGeorge Bundy, Jonathan Crowe, and Sidney Drell] ask of them a greater measure of openness about their real nuclear capabilities, suggesting that each in different ways pays a heavy price for its pretense—a pretense that, in any event, has worn irritatingly thin. . . . The advantage of recognizing these countries for what they are is not merely a matter of dealing with reality, as important as that is. 'It is also a matter of *not* dealing with these countries as they are *not*.'"

34. There is a vast critique of deterrence. But see Jonathan Schell's *The Abolition* (New York: Knopf, 1984) for a profound and passionate critique of nuclear weapons and deterrence. For an Indian philosopher's view, see Bimal Krishna Matilal's

"Between Peace and Deterrence," in *Peace Studies: The Hard Questions*, ed. Elaine Kaye, Oxford Peace Lectures 1984–85 (London: Rex Collings, 1987), 59–82.

35. This line of argumentation draws on John Lewis Gaddis, *The Long Peace: Inquiries Into the History of the Cold War* (New York: Oxford Univ. Press, 1987), chapter 8.

36. Glenn Snyder long ago alluded to this in his formulation of the "stability-instability paradox": stability at the nuclear level would permit instability at lower levels. See his *Deterrence and Defense: Towards a Theory of National Security* (Princeton, N.J.: Princeton Univ. Press, 1961). This is also hinted at in P.M.S. Blackett, *Fear, War, and the Bomb* (New York: Whittlesey House/McGraw Hill Book Company, 1948), 203: "On the other hand the threat of use of weapons of mass destruction may prove far less a deterrent than an incitement of the rival power to strengthen its position by relatively unprovocative means. In fact, the obvious counter to the diplomatic use of the threat of atomic and similar weapons is the intensification of political warfare, or the actual waging of a guerilla type of war."

37. This recalls Raju Thomas' point that, if both sides go nuclear, India will have lost the advantage of more or less permanent conventional military superiority.

38. See for instance the Atomic Energy Act of 1948, the reconstitution of the Atomic Energy Commission (AEC) in 1958, and the AEC Act of 1962.

39. Raju Thomas argues that the nuclear weapons option is used to justify a civilian nuclear program that could at best meet only 10 percent of India's future energy needs. See his "India," in *Energy and Security in the Industrializing World*, eds. Raju G.C. Thomas and Bennett Ramberg (Lexington, K.Y.: The University Press of Kentucky, 1990), 13–34.

40. There have been a number of accidents and failures at Indian nuclear plants since 1993. The most publicized was the fire at Narora in March 1994 which led to the temporary closing of the plant. The Indian government has apparently begun a program of cooperation with the U.S. on nuclear safety issues. Eight U.S. officials from the Nuclear Regulatory Commission (NRC) visited the Kaiga, Narora, and Tarapur plants in mid-February 1995.

3

Status Quo: Maintaining Nuclear Ambiguity

Aabha Dixit

India's nuclear policy has been perceived and described, especially in the West, as one of "strategic ambiguity." India espouses global nuclear disarmament but maintains a de facto weapons capability and keeps the nuclear option open. The ambiguous element surrounding this policy has been deliberate and calculated. Traditionally, any policy approach that seeks to hold the middle ground runs the risk of facing a two-front attack. This axiom also holds true for India's nuclear policy because it has sought to develop a prudent mix between idealism and a "principled position" on the one hand and pragmatism on the other. In the five decades since the atomic energy program began under the stewardship of India's first prime minister, Jawaharlal Nehru, this policy approach has striven to be a combination of a sense of idealism that world peace must be predicated upon nuclear disarmament and the belief that national security considerations demand the availability of all options to resist any threat. While these two tracks of the policy have not developed simultaneously, they, nevertheless, have become conjoined since the late 1970s to form an approach that receives support among the intellectual elite, political parties, academics, and common citizens. The results of the Kroc Institute poll confirm this, showing 57 percent of respondents in favor of official government policy. While India's approach to nuclear disarmament has remained relatively stable over the years, its nuclear nonproliferation stance, which has been subsumed under the larger disarmament framework, has shifted. With Pakistan's attempt to develop nuclear weapons assuming an overt character beginning in the 1980s, New Delhi's nuclear nonproliferation policies have revolved around the Pakistan factor. This has occurred partly because of New Delhi's own policies of playing up the Pakistan threat. Strategic thinkers in the West have focused on the potential nuclear confrontation in the region and have urged the two countries, so far unsuccessfully, to sign the Nuclear Nonproliferation Treaty (NPT).

The centrality of Pakistan in Indian strategic perceptions is confirmed in the Kroc Institute poll, where concern about Pakistani nuclear capabilities is seen as much greater than the threat from China. The Kroc poll also shows the widespread unwillingness in India to renounce its nuclear option and to sign the NPT in the context of global or bilateral disarmament.

Historical Evolution of the Policy

1945 to 1960

Coherence and continuity have marked India's nuclear disarmament stance. Mahatma Gandhi, who led a remarkable moral campaign against the British imperialists, saw the development of the atom bomb as "deadening the finest feeling that has sustained mankind for ages."[1] In the same article, Gandhi said, "the moral to be legitimately drawn from the supreme tragedy of the bomb is that it will not be destroyed by counterbombs even as violence cannot be by counterviolence. Mankind has to get out of violence only through nonviolence."[2] In another piece in the journal *Harijan*, Gandhi said, "I regard the employment of the atom bomb for the wholesale destruction of men, women and children as the most diabolical use of science."[3] Gandhi's moral opposition to the atom bomb has long guided New Delhi's consistent call for nuclear disarmament.

With Gandhi's philosophy of nonviolence undergirding India's nuclear policy, his chosen political disciple, Jawaharlal Nehru, articulated this policy with great fervor. Addressing the United Nations General Assembly session in Paris on 3 November 1948, Nehru evoked the Gandhian theme to underscore India's moral opposition to the development of nuclear weapons. He told the assembly that "I am not afraid of the bigness of great powers, and their armies, their fleets and their atom bombs. That is the lesson which my Master [Gandhi] taught me. We stood as an unarmed people against a great country and a powerful empire."[4]

Despite the moral appeal of India's nuclear policy, Nehru faced a serious dilemma. As a Western-educated statesman influenced by a desire to harness technology for national progress, Nehru sought to master nuclear energy for peaceful purposes. For many at the time, achievement in the field of nuclear science was a "symbol of India's march into the modern age."[5] Through the creation of the Atomic Energy Commission (AEC) in 1948, Nehru sought to control nuclear technology and channel research into technologies that would seek to lift the standard of living of the Indian people. That same year Nehru selected Dr. Homi Bhabha, the architect of India's atomic energy program, to take charge of the AEC's functioning. Previously, in 1945, Bhabha had been able to persuade the House of Tatas to establish the Tata Institute for Fundamental Research in Bombay. In 1962 the Indian Parliament passed the Atomic Energy Act, formally authorizing the AEC to "produce, develop, use, and dispose of atomic energy and carry out research into any matter connected therewith" and to harness atomic energy for "the welfare of the people of India" and for "other peaceful purposes."[6]

In the early 1950s, two themes dominated India's nuclear policy. First, having made the development of an infrastructure for atomic energy a symbol of the country's independence and capability to invigorate and modernize itself, Nehru argued at all international and national fora that the orientation of atomic programs should be exclusively focused on peaceful purposes. The second point he stressed was the retention of national control over atomic programs. He strongly attacked all attempts at setting up an international authority to regulate the development of nuclear energy, referring to such plans as "atomic colonialism" and criticized the major powers for their continued belief that nuclear weapons would bring greater security. Nehru also sought to highlight the urgency of nuclear disarmament. In 1954 he proposed a "Standstill Agreement" among the nuclear weapons states. In a 2 April speech before Parliament Nehru urged the nuclear weapons powers, pending progress toward elimination of weapons of mass destruction, to discontinue production and stockpiling of nuclear weapons, to inform world public opinion about the destructive power of these weapons, and to raise the issue within the UN Disarmament Commission. Nehru also urged peoples and countries around the world to raise their voices against the production of these weapons.[7]

This period could be characterized as one of intense idealism. Krishna Menon, Nehru's confidant, amply reflected the government's policy in his speeches at the UN: its concerns about the effects of radiation from nuclear weapons tests, its fears about the temptation by nuclear weapons states to use nuclear weapons in conflict situations, and the belief that nuclear weapons bring no additional security. Nehru even commissioned the Defence Science Organisation in 1955 to study the consequences of nuclear weapons use.[8] These findings were later presented to the UN General Assembly by Krishna Menon. During this period, India presented eight separate disarmament initiatives, either individually or jointly, within various bodies of the UN. These included: a draft resolution on "Peaceful Uses of Atomic Energy," submitted to the General Assembly at its third session in 1948; a draft resolution on "Declaration on the Removal of the Threat of a New War and the Strengthening of Peace and Security Among Nations" at the fourth session in 1949; communication of the Standstill Agreement and proposals contained therein to the UN secretary general on 8 April 1954; inclusion of the item "Dissemination of Information on the Effects of Atomic Radiation and on the Effects of Experimental Explosions of Thermonuclear Bombs" at the tenth session in

1955; note verbale from the Indian representative at the UN to the chairman of the Disarmament Commission proposing steps for "Cessation of All Explosions of Nuclear and Other Weapons," 25 July 1956; a draft resolution on the "Composition of the Disarmament Commission" at the twelfth session in 1958; a request for an agenda item "Suspension of Nuclear and Thermonuclear Tests" at the fourteenth session in 1959; and a draft resolution, "Directives on General and Complete Disarmament," also at the fourteenth session, 1959.

By the mid-to-late 1950s, there was a slight shift in the Indian government's position. This partly reflected changes taking place in the international arena. With the Soviet Union having achieved thermonuclear capability and with mutual deterrence coming into place, there was a realization in Moscow and Washington, despite their other differences, that nuclear weapons technology should not proliferate to other countries. The U.S. and USSR began to cooperate to prevent the horizontal spread of nuclear weapons. In 1957 they worked together to create the International Atomic Energy Agency (IAEA) and in 1963 they signed the Partial Test Ban Treaty (PTBT). India supported the establishment of the IAEA and signed the PTBT. At the time some criticized the government's decisions on grounds that it had succumbed to international pressures designed to rein in developing countries through technology restrictions. But New Delhi held that a PTBT, if universalized, could contribute in some small measure to nuclear disarmament. It supported the IAEA because the statute of the agency sought to promote peaceful uses of nuclear technology without discrimination. Growing out of then U.S. president Eisenhower's "Atoms for Peace" plan, the IAEA was designed "to accelerate and enlarge the contribution of atomic energy to peace, health and prosperity throughout the world" (Article II of the IAEA Statute). India argued that the IAEA could not be used to deny technology to any state wishing to pursue peaceful uses or become the nuclear nonproliferation watchdog (a role that the West has increasingly sought for the IAEA, especially since the Gulf War, as it has introduced measures for the more stringent—if selective—application of nuclear safeguards).

Despite these slight shifts in emphasis, India's early nuclear policy continued to be premised upon:

- a sense of idealism that drew sustenance from Gandhi's belief that war and violence are morally repugnant and that the way to truth is through nonviolence;
- an understanding that nuclear weapons are an extension of the philosophy of violence and therefore need to be countered by nuclear disarmament;
- a belief that the peaceful uses of nuclear technology can benefit the

community and therefore should be pursued with zeal;
- a conviction that the pursuit of peaceful uses of nuclear technology should remain within the domain of individual countries, with apex bodies like IAEA helping to promote and assist research on a nondiscriminatory basis.

While the nuclear issue dominated much of India's foreign policy, there was no apparent correlation between nuclear policy and national security concerns. There were several reasons for this disjunction. Most important, none of India's neighbors had gone nuclear and the prospects for them doing so in the 1950s and early 1960s, with the exception of China, appeared remote. A small pro-bomb lobby existed within India, but its argumentation revolved around the prestige that nuclear weapons would presumably bring rather than any specific security threat.[9] In the debates about nuclear weapons from 1945 to 1960, no single country-specific threat existed. The danger that did exist seemed distant, and was more global in scale. The nuclear weapons option was not judged on specific security considerations, but on the larger philosophical grounds of Gandhian moralism and the principle of universality.

Some commentators argue that Nehru's policy was more realist than idealistic and that the nuclear option was deliberately kept open during the 1950s.[10] Rodney Jones believes that Bhabha, who had the ear of the prime minister and was a known pro-bomb advocate, may have convinced Nehru to keep the option open for weaponization.[11] The principal concern cited was a potential threat from China.

Such arguments underestimate the importance of nuclear disarmament concerns for Nehru's foreign policy, which aspired to moral leadership among nonaligned developing nations. It is also important to note that the capability for weaponization apparently existed long before it was exercised. Bhabha asserted as early as 1948 that India could produce a bomb, but the test of that capability did not come until 1974. As for the threat from China, this did not yet loom large in the 1950s, certainly not in a nuclear dimension, and therefore there was no reason to consider the nuclear weapons option. Further, in keeping with its general line of disarmament, nondiscrimination, and universality, India offered the UN in 1960 detailed "directives" for general and complete disarmament, plans which would have closed its option along with those of all other countries, including the nuclear powers.[12]

1961 to 1974

The phase between 1961 and 1974 proved to be tumultuous, as the principles governing India's nuclear policy came under attack from both flanks. It was a period when India's global disarmament approach could not keep pace with changing events and began to fade. Only four disarmament initiatives were presented to the UN during this period.[13] The weakening of ties to China, which ended with the border war of 1962 and which was followed by the Chinese nuclear test in Lop Nor in October 1964, forced a change in the Nehruvian model. The previous approach was perceived as having brought no tangible benefit to Indian security. The security debate in India began to consider the nuclear option. Meanwhile, negotiations on the Nuclear Nonproliferation Treaty in the UN's Eighteen Nation Disarmament Commission created additional tensions that led to calls for reappraising nuclear policy.

The worsening of relations with China began in the late 1950s and peaked with the border war. The defeat at the hands of the Chinese in 1962 strengthened the case of those opposing the Nehruvian model. They argued that high-profile moral diplomacy had not prevented China from crushing Indian military forces on the ground and weakening India's international prestige. Realpolitik demanded a thorough review of the country's security policy, including consideration of the atomic bomb option. The Chinese test at Lop Nor two years later cemented this trend. While no correlation has been established between Beijing's decision to explode the nuclear weapon in 1964 and its adverse relationship with India, these two factors certainly combined to influence Indian nuclear policy. The argument for weaponization, or at least leaving the option open, gained new legitimacy and support.

If the Chinese defeat brought into public the pro-bomb lobby,[14] the NPT negotiations which began at this time weakened the position of the no-bomb lobby.[15] Those who wanted India to sign the NPT irrespective of limitations were put on the defensive by the discriminatory nonproliferation agenda then emerging among the major powers. The Western countries were seeking to highlight the nth country proliferation problem rather than the continuing and accelerating accumulation of weapons by the major powers. The idea of a universal commitment to nuclear weapons elimination gave way to a plan for preventing the acquisition of nuclear capability by "other" nations. Canada, which had signed a safeguards-free nuclear agreement with China in the 1950s, began to express concerns, without documentation, that India might divert plutonium from Canadian-supplied reactors for military purposes.[16] Although Canada did not withdraw from its nuclear agreements, the raising of such questions in a multilateral forum implied severe criticism of India's nuclear program. Such concerns also revealed the NPT agenda to be focused on horizontal proliferation rather than vertical proliferation, thus reflecting the interests of major powers like the United States rather than developing nations like India.

Status Quo: Maintaining Nuclear Ambiguity

As the bomb debate became more complicated, the Congress governments of Prime Ministers Lal Bahadur Shastri and Indira Gandhi created the first shift in policy after the Nehru years. Although the shift was not large, it nevertheless provided future governments the necessary opening to create an all-encompassing nuclear policy. Soon after the Chinese explosion, Prime Minister Shastri inaugurated the policy of ambiguity by declaring that India had the capability to make nuclear weapons, but that the government was not keen to exercise this option. At the same time, it kept its option open on conducting a peaceful nuclear explosion.[17] Internationally, the shifting focus of Indian nuclear policy centered on the Eighteen Nation Disarmament Commission, where the Irish draft resolution of 1959 had set the ball rolling for NPT negotiations. Over the years that the NPT was debated in Geneva, the Indian position showed a gradual strengthening of arguments against any discriminatory form of nuclear nonproliferation.

Accompanying these shifts in foreign policy was an intensifying political debate at home. The immediate post-Nehru years witnessed particularly sharp discussions. The pro-bomb lobby grew and became more vigorous. Some Western writers have sought to explain this growth as a logical culmination of younger scientists and researchers coming into senior positions by the mid-1960s, which also coincided with the relative maturity of the atomic energy program. They have quoted Homi Bhabha's talk on All India Radio on 24 October 1964 shortly after the Chinese nuclear test, as evidence that the pro-bomb lobby among the scientists had grown strong and was ready to assume a public image. In this speech, Bhabha declared that "the explosion of a nuclear device by China is a signal that there is no time to be lost" and added that "The only defense against [nuclear] attack appears to be a capability and threat of retaliation."[18]

While the Hindu nationalist parties like the Jan Sangh advocated the development of nuclear weapons, the Swatantra Party took the other end of the spectrum by demanding that India sign the NPT. The Socialists, Communists, and Congress took intermediate positions, favoring a middle-ground approach of neither renouncing nor advocating nuclear weapons but keeping the option open. Some political leaders declared their opposition to nuclear weapons but urged that the option be kept open with a special reservation that it could be energized should the country ever face a clear and present danger.

A 1968 poll conducted in the four major cities (New Delhi, Bombay, Madras, and Calcutta) showed strong but qualified public support for the nuclear option. Seventy-nine percent of those polled favored an independent nuclear capability. However, when the same question was worded to note the cuts in development spending which an Indian nuclear program would bring, the results showed lower support bases for a nuclear capability. Indian public opinion wanted to see the nuclear weapon as part of the country's "prestige," but this attitude was tempered by a sense of realism over the potential economic costs of such a policy.[19]

Pressured by the pro- and no-bomb lobbies, and grappling with what decision to take on the NPT, the Indira Gandhi government opted for the middle ground. The government issued a statement reiterating India's traditional condemnation of nuclear weapons but also leaving the option open, arguing that weaponization should never be ruled out. The prime minister also announced New Delhi's decision not to sign the NPT, because of the treaty's inherently discriminatory character. Her statement to the Indian Parliament on 24 April 1968 sought to placate everyone—leftists, right-wing nationalists, academics, scientists, and intellectuals:

> [Our] policy is framed after due consideration of the national interest, specifically with regard to national security ... this policy, as well as all policies bearing on security, is kept under constant review. But we do feel that the events of the last twenty years clearly show that the possession of nuclear weapons have not given any military advantage in situations of bitter armed conflict.
>
> We think that nuclear weapons are no substitute for military preparedness involving the conventional weapons. The choice before us involves not only the question of making a few atom bombs, but of engaging in an arms race with sophisticated nuclear warheads and an effective missile delivery system. Such a course, I do not think would strengthen national security. On the other hand, it may well endanger our internal security by imposing a very heavy economic burden which would be in addition to the present expenditure on defence. Nothing will serve the interests of those who are hostile to us than for us to lose our sense of perspective and to undertake measures which would undermine the basic progress of the country.[20]

Indira Gandhi's statement showed how keen the government was to ensure broad-based support for its nuclear policy. The new approach was sensitive to public opinion—implying a capability for weaponization yet avoiding the associated economic costs that might impede development. India would avoid getting into a nuclear arms race, but by staying a few notches away from overt weaponization, it would retain the latitude of changing course in the future. In an earlier debate in Parliament, Mrs. Gandhi had categorically declared "we have stated that the Government for India does not propose to manufacture nuclear weapons. This is a decision taken many years ago and is unrelated to the treaty on nonproliferation of nuclear weapons."[21] Nonetheless, a major threshold had been passed, as New Delhi moved toward the development and testing of a nuclear device.

Pokhran and Beyond

The 1974 nuclear test at Pokhran, in the great Indian desert in the state of Rajasthan, was greeted with alarm in the West but it did not substantially alter India's stance on nuclear issues. Many Westerners feared that India was on its way to overt weaponization. Others felt that even if India's assurance of not weaponizing were to be believed, it now had to be considered a de facto sixth nuclear weapons state. The test seriously set back the nuclear power program, as it caused Canada to withdraw cooperation and the U.S. to strengthen its technology restriction regimes. Contrary to what some Westerners suggested, the Pokhran test was not intended to undermine the NPT. Had India opted for that route, the explosion would have occurred much earlier, when India possessed the capability and a test could have grievously hurt the NPT in its infancy. India's policy remained the same during and after the test period as it was before testing: denunciation of the nuclear arms race, opposition to the NPT, denial of any intention to build nuclear weapons, but a refusal to foreclose the nuclear option in the future.

Many reasons have been ascribed for the decision to conduct the Pokhran test. They range from powerful pressures exerted by the scientific lobby to validate their achievements to Mrs. Gandhi's suspected attempt to divert domestic attention from the anti-Congress movement that was then gaining ground in Gujarat and Bihar. It is also assumed that Mrs. Gandhi wanted to demonstrate India's coming-of-age as a major international player and at the very least a significant regional power. Whatever the exact motivations for the test, the immediate political result was an increase in support for India's nuclear policy among domestic audiences. Support for the government's nuclear policy became an accepted fact for all political parties. Even Prime Minister Morarji Desai, despite his personal predilections, was not able to change the basic thrust of policy. Addressing the first special session of the UN General Assembly devoted to disarmament in 1978, Morarji Desai evoked Gandhian values of nonviolence and sought to give a different nuance to the policy. He said,

> I should like to refer to the Nuclear Non-Proliferation Treaty. India is among those who have not signed this treaty. There has been considerable misunderstanding of our motives. To remove these, I should like to declare that we yield to none in our commitment to comprehensive disarmament. We are the only country that has pledged not to manufacture or acquire nuclear weapons even if the rest of the world did so. I solemnly reiterate that pledge before this august Assembly. In fact, we have gone further and abjured

nuclear explosions even for peaceful purposes. We ask from others no more than the self-restraint we impose upon ourselves. But our objection to the Treaty is because it is so patently discriminatory. It makes an invidious distinction between countries having nuclear weaponry and those devoted to the pursuit of nuclear research and technology entirely for peaceful purposes.[22]

Clearly Desai refused to renounce the option, while making very unambiguous pledges not to manufacture or acquire nuclear weapons or conduct nuclear tests. Desai carefully distinguished between the Indian government's opposition to the NPT and the possibility of a nuclear option for itself.

Perhaps the greatest impact of the Pokhran test was its influence on the Pakistani nuclear program. This is not the place for a detailed discussion of Pakistani nuclear developments, but the immediate result of India's test was unmistakable: a determination in Islamabad to get the bomb. This in turn introduced the Pakistani factor into Indian nuclear planning and profoundly altered the policy debate. An overweening obsession with Pakistan's nuclear program began to grip New Delhi and by the 1980s and 1990s came to dominate public thinking on these issues. The finding of the Kroc Institute poll that Indian concern about a Pakistani nuclear threat far outweighs other security considerations reflects the evolution of a trend in public perception that began in the 1970s. The emergence of a de facto arms competition in South Asia obscured India's traditional commitment to global disarmament and added new force to the pro-bomb lobby. While New Delhi managed to retain its commitment to disarmament, and even launched several new international initiatives in this regard, the Pakistani factor served as a constant distraction from the Gandhian/Nehruvian ideal.

The Pakistani factor attracted greater attention after 1980 and complicated India's long-standing stress on global disarmament. With growing reports about Pakistan's attempts to achieve nuclear weapons capability, the security dimension in the nuclear policy debate received greater attention, with a corresponding de-emphasis of disarmament policies. The Pakistan factor began to envelope New Delhi's nuclear policies, assuming ever larger dimensions. This was especially true after the reelection of Mrs. Gandhi as prime minister in 1980. Clandestine Pakistani nuclear weapons activities were highlighted, as were the activities of the scientist Dr. Abdul Qadir Khan and his "theft" of critical secrets regarding enrichment technology from the Dutch firm of URENCO.[23] Attention increasingly focused on the emerging nearby threat in Pakistan.

The previous themes of Indian nuclear policy were not lost, however, and continued to appear in major international fora. Then External Affairs Minister P.V. Narasimha Rao repeated New Delhi's critique of the NPT in 1982 at the second special session of the UN General Assembly devoted to disarmament:

> ... it is a bizarre game which the world is witnessing today in the name of disarmament. The effort is, in fact, to move towards more armaments rather than less. ... One wonders, then, whether the game of disarmament in the nuclear age is, *inter alia,* an effort by the great Powers to control smaller countries—shall we say one of the modern versions of colonialism and imperialism? In the same manner, all too often the focus has been on horizontal proliferation, as if to suggest that nuclear weapons in the possession of certain chosen States are somehow permissible or safe, but that they should not be allowed to fall into the hands of others. ... Unfortunately, the [Nuclear] Non-Proliferation Treaty, as it emerged, was based on the faulty notion of checking horizontal proliferation alone without placing simultaneous and equal curbs on the existing nuclear-weapon States.[24]

Indian leaders also continued to speak out for global disarmament, often issuing calls for the elimination of all nuclear weapons within a time-bound framework. The most detailed and ambitious of these proposals was that of Rajiv Gandhi who issued his Action Plan to Usher in a Nuclear Weapon Free and Non-Violent World Order at the third UN Special Session on Disarmament in 1988.[25] The Action Plan, which sought to link all elements on the disarmament agenda, called upon all nuclear weapons states to reach agreement for eliminating their nuclear arsenals by a certain date (year 2010). Simultaneously, it called upon threshold states not to cross over the nuclear threshold. The Action Plan also called for a nuclear test ban, a freeze on the production of fissile materials, and a treaty that would prohibit both the use and the threat of use of nuclear weapons. The plan was an attempt by India to widen the disarmament debate. It was also a way of easing political pressures, both domestic and international, that were building up for and against the prospect of an Indian nuclear option.

In the 1990s, following the demise of the Soviet Union and the end of bloc politics, India's nuclear debate has focused increasingly on the possible presence of nuclear weapons in South Asia and continuing opposition to the NPT. The NPT debate was fine-tuned, under pressure from the United States and Russia, with alternate arrangements like the 3 + 2 regional nonproliferation proposal put forward by Washington. The proposal envisaged India and Pakistan locking themselves into a bilateral nuclear nonproliferation agreement, with the U.S., Russia, and China as external guarantors. This was later amended to become the 5 + 2 + 2 proposal, which would have included the five permanent UN Security Council members (China, France, U.K., Russia, and the U.S.), Japan and

Germany, along with India and Pakistan. The construct remained bilateral, with seven external guarantors. But India's policy continued to reject such constricted approaches. At the Security Council's summit meeting in New York on 31 January 1992, Prime Minister P.V. Narasimha Rao emphasized the theme of the Action Plan and suggested that in view of the positive developments, resulting from the end of the cold war and ongoing nuclear reductions, the target date for a nuclear weapon-free world should be advanced to the end of the present century.

India's disarmament initiatives were muted, however, by the continuing controversy over possible nuclear weapons in South Asia. In addition, Pakistan made frequent counterproposals that contributed to Western perceptions of a dichotomy between India's global disarmament message and the realities of South Asia. Pakistan suggested such proposals as the establishment of a nuclear weapon-free zone in South Asia, simultaneous acceptance of IAEA full-scope safeguards, mutual inspection of each other's nuclear facilities, a bilateral test ban, and most recently, the idea of a five-nation meeting (U.S., Russia, China, India, and Pakistan). India rejected these proposals on grounds that they were conceived in the narrow context of South Asia, ignoring the global reach of the nuclear disarmament issue. New Delhi perceived the Pakistani suggestions as providing propaganda mileage to Islamabad while diverting attention from its clandestine nuclear weapons program.

Pakistan's nuclear weapons program is not the only major security concern for Indian policymakers. They also point to continuing concerns about the Chinese nuclear arsenals, the presence of nuclear weapons in the Indian Ocean, and new uncertainties and prospects of proliferation arising out of the breakup of the former USSR. Reports about the smuggling of nuclear materials and lucrative offers of employment for former nuclear scientists are highly unsettling. Because of the geographic proximity of the Central Asian Republics, continuing uncertainty over the control of strategic and tactical nuclear weapons and nuclear materials, technology and scientific personnel have made proliferation concerns a major priority for India, especially in light of the rising trend of Islamic reassertion in this part of the world and possible linkages that can be established by Pakistan. Evidence of cooperation between China and Pakistan in the nuclear field has also surfaced from time to time. All of these factors are cited as reasons by New Delhi for keeping the nuclear option open.

Nuclear nonproliferation continues to figure prominently on the international and regional disarmament agenda, and was a major priority during the time of the Nuclear Nonprofliferation Treaty Extension/Review Conference in 1995. India's position on the issue remains the same. Prime Minister Narasimha Rao however had made it clear during the Security Council summit meeting in January 1992 that the proliferation threat can be addressed only within the framework of a new international consensus. This consensus would have to be based upon a universal, comprehensive, and nondiscriminatory regime linked to the goal of complete elimination of nuclear weapons. This theme was reiterated in the Indian Parliament in May 1994, when the prime minister spoke about the willingness of India to participate in the Nuclear Nonproliferation Treaty Extension/Review Conference as an observer if the conference would be willing to commit itself to a universal disarmament regime. The NPT conference focused predominantly on the indefinite extension of the existing treaty rather than the negotiation of a new disarmament instrument, and so New Delhi decided not to send a delegation to the gathering. India thus remains one of only a handful of countries, along with Pakistan and Israel, that stands outside the NPT regime.

India has always made a distinction between the NPT and nonproliferation. While maintaining reservations on the former, India is fully committed to the goal of curbing nuclear proliferation. It maintains that selective preventive or punitive actions will not achieve the desired results. A new global nonproliferation regime must be crafted. It must be universal, comprehensive, and nondiscriminatory, and linked to the goal of complete elimination of nuclear weapons. Flowing from this consideration, India is unwilling to renounce its nuclear option until there is a global commitment to universal nonproliferation and disarmament. The results of the Kroc Institute survey show that this official perspective is shared by a large proportion of the Indian elite: Fifty-eight percent of those supporting India's current policy and 42 percent of those favoring its development of nuclear weapons cited a time-bound plan for global nuclear disarmament as a condition for India's renunciation of nuclear weapons.

Conclusion

India's nuclear policy has been the subject of great concern in the West, where it is variously termed contradictory, ambiguous, and paradoxical. The comments of Rodney Jones are typical:

> India has opposed nuclear weapons in principle and advocated both nuclear disarmament and nonproliferation. Yet India staunchly refused to join the [Nuclear] Non-Proliferation Treaty and even dealt a serious blow to the objectives of the treaty by detonating a nuclear explosive device in May 1974.[26]

Added to these Western concerns has been the parallel development of ballistic missile technology. New Delhi denies any possible linkage between missile capability and the nuclear option. There is strong apprehension in the West that taken together, the two components represent a significant nuclear capability and a major threat to regional security. The existence of unsafeguarded facilities in India has caused additional concern in the West, raising the possibility that New Delhi may be accumulating stocks of weapons-grade plutonium.

The other elements of India's nuclear policy, especially its global outlook and commitment to universal disarmament, carry little conviction in the West. They are often dismissed as mere utopianism or as a cover for more sinister motives. Yet these lofty principles have important meaning for India's leaders and the public. India's nuclear policies have evolved over the years in response to international pressures and changing conditions, but the underlying philosophy crafted under the influence of Gandhi and Nehru has prevented steps toward overt weaponization. Such a policy would not fit into the national ethos. It is perhaps the only area where all Indian governments, irrespective of their political affiliations, have evolved a broad policy consensus. Nonetheless, the continuity of India's disarmament message and credibility of its "holdall" approach to the nuclear option have gradually eroded in recent years. The agenda has narrowed, and the popular perception in India and abroad is that the nuclear option is premised on the threat from Pakistan. Similarly, New Delhi's opposition to the NPT is seen by some as the main plank of the country's nuclear policy. This undue emphasis on opposition to the NPT and the nuclear threat from Pakistan has blurred the underlying principles of India's nuclear policy and created uncertainties and tensions for the future.

Notes

1. M.K. Gandhi, "Atom Bomb and Ahimsa," *Harijan* (Poona), 7 July 1946.
2. Ibid.
3. M.K. Gandhi, "With an English Journalist," *Harijan* (New Delhi), 29 September 1946.
4. Jawaharlal Nehru, *India's Foreign Policy, Select Speeches, September 1946 to April 1961*, Publications Division, Ministry of Space Information and Broadcasting, Government of India, New Delhi, 1961, 162.
5. Girilal Jain, "India," chap. 5A in *Non Proliferation: The Why and the Wherefore*, ed. Jozef Goldblat (London: SIPRI/Taylor and Francis, 1985), 89.
6. India, Acts of Parliament 1963, (New Delhi, 1963).
7. Nehru, *India's Foreign Policy, Select Speeches*, 187.
8. Government of India, *Nuclear Explosions and Their Effects*, New Delhi, June 1956; October 1958.
9. This rationale continues to predominate among elite respondents to the Kroc Institute survey who favored the development of nuclear weapons, as their most common response to the question of why India should develop nuclear weapons, following the Pakistani nuclear threat (57 percent), was to improve India's bargaining power in the world (44 percent).

10. Western analysts suggest that the peaceful element of India's nuclear program was merely a facade to cloak the covert development of atomic weapons.

11. Rodney Jones, "India," chap. 5B in *Non Proliferation: The Why and the Wherefore*, ed. Jozeph Goldblat (London: SIPRI/Taylor and Francis, 1985), 107.

12. Draft resolution presented by India and eleven other nations 15 November 1960, which was unanimously adopted at the UN General Assembly Fourteenth Session; Document No. A/C. 1/L. 259 and Add. 1–2.

13. These were: a draft resolution "Question of Disarmament" introduced at the Sixteenth UN General Assembly Session, 1961; a request for the agenda item "The Urgent Need for Suspension of Nuclear and Thermo-Nuclear Tests" 9 July 1962; a request for the agenda item "Non-Proliferation of Nuclear Weapons" 10 October 1964; and Resolution 2028 presented by India and seven other nations "A Treaty to Prevent the Proliferation of Nuclear Weapons," Twentieth Session, 1965.

14. The pro-bomb lobby included political parties like the Jan Sangh, scientists like Bhabha, and civil servants like K. Subrahmanyam, C.S. Jha, and V.C. Trivedi; quoted from Ashok Kapur, *India's Nuclear Option: Atomic Diplomacy and Decision Making* (New York: Praeger, 1976), 145–52.

15. The no-bomb lobby included political parties like the Swatantra Party, and civil servants like L.K. Jha and M.J. Desai. Even mainstream politicians in the ruling Congress Party imbued with Gandhian values, like Morarji Desai and Lal Bahadur Shastri, were leaning toward the no-bomb argument.

16. Girilal Jain, "India," 91.

17. Kapur, *India's Nuclear Option*, 134.

18. J.P. Jain, *Nuclear India*, vol. 2 (New Delhi: Radiant Publishers, 1974), 139–45.

19. Kapur, *India's Nuclear Option*, 180–81. Three other polls that were conducted in the pre-Pokhran period and quoted by the author include Gerard Braunthal's elite poll whose results were published in his article "An Attitude Survey in India," *Public Opinion Quarterly* 33, no. 1 (Spring 1969), 81; and two studies by the Indian Institute of Public Opinion, in October 1968 and December 1971.

20. Indira Gandhi, statement in Parliament, Lok Sabha Debate, 24 April 1968; J. P. Jain, *Nuclear India*, 201–202.

21. Indira Gandhi, statement in Parliament, 5 April 1968.

22. Morarji Desai, speech delivered at the Special Session of the UN General Assembly, New York, 9 June 1978.

23. See Leonard S. Spector with Jacqueline R. Smith, *Nuclear Ambitions: The Spread of Nuclear Weapons, 1989–90* (Boulder, Colo.: Westview, 1990) for details of Pakistan's nuclear program.

24. P.V. Narasimha Rao, Twelfth Special Session of the UN General Assembly, Ninth Plenary Meeting (Second Special Session on Disarmament), New York, 11 June 1982.

25. Government of India, *Disarmament: India's Initiatives*, Ministry of External Affairs, New Delhi, 1988.

26. Jones, "India," 101.

4

Freeze: Halting the Testing and Development of Nuclear Weapons

Sumit Ganguly

In this chapter the term "freeze" is used interchangeably with the term "capping." No explicit definition of a nuclear "cap" exists in the South Asian context. Few internal debates, in fact, have taken place in India about the range of possible options that the country may pursue regarding nuclear weapons.[1] Despite the absence of an informed public debate on the technical and political dimensions of a freeze, it is nevertheless possible to identify the key technical components of the freeze option. Three elements are critical: accession to a test ban treaty, a verifiable cutoff of weapons-grade fissile material production, and the provision of International Atomic Energy Agency (IAEA) safeguards over relevant nuclear activities.

Maximizing the political viability of such an option in the Indian context would entail making it nondiscriminatory. Consequently, this paper envisions that a freeze would involve multilateral implementation beyond the subcontinent. The immediate concerns of this paper, however, are the nuclear programs of India and Pakistan.

The South Asian Security Environment

Any analysis of the prospects of an Indian nuclear freeze needs to be grounded in a discussion of the security environment on the subcontinent. This must include an analysis of the policies of India's principal potential adversaries, Pakistan and China.

Since independence in 1947, India has fought three wars with Pakistan in 1947–48, 1965, and 1971, and one with the People's Republic of China in 1962.[2] In 1987 India and Pakistan almost plunged into a fourth war over a crisis stemming from mutual misconceptions that grew out of the conduct of "Brasstacks," independent India's largest military exercise.[3] In 1990, yet another crisis punctuated India/Pakistan relations, one whose precise dimensions remain murky. In late 1990 the Kashmiri insurgency had peaked. Frustrated with their inability to control infiltration across the mountainous border with Kashmir, Indian decision makers contemplated striking into Pakistani territory to destroy encampments being used to train Kashmiri insurgents. Fearing an Indian onslaught, the Pakistani leadership contemplated military action, including the use of nuclear weapons.[4]

Although India's relations with China are improving, the border dispute remains unresolved.[5] In September 1993 the two countries signed an important agreement which, among other matters, significantly broadened the existing band of confidence-building measures (CBMs) designed to avoid inadvertent conflict along the Himalayan border.[6] Though Indian decision makers are loath to admit it publicly, the Sino-Indian border agreement of 1993 signaled India's acquiescence to the Chinese territorial gains of 1962. A formal, legal border settlement is still to be negotiated, but India has in effect conceded Chinese claims in the western sector near Tibet.

The Sino-Indian relationship, though not overtly conflictual, remains competitive. Nor is this likely to change in the foreseeable future. China and India both have self-images as great powers within Asia and beyond. Yet they have markedly divergent political systems, and only on occasion do they support the same causes. Any convergence of interests is typically fleeting.[7] Despite the recent warmth in Sino-Indian relations, New Delhi remains wary about China's long-term goals and intentions. China's involvement in northern Burma and its attempts to obtain port facilities on the Burmese coast of the Bay of Bengal have heightened the anxieties of India's decision makers.[8] Consequently, New Delhi will continue to approach its northern neighbor with a degree of circumspection. However, it is unlikely that India will embark on a ballistic missile race with China. Nevertheless, it will, subject to domestic fiscal constraints and international political pressures, continue the testing of short- and intermediate-range rockets like the *Prithvi* and the *Agni*.[9] At another level, India will seek to extend existing confidence-building measures along the Sino-Indian border to ensure "peace and tranquillity"—to borrow a term from official parlance.

For the near term, then, Pakistan will remain India's principal security problem. The results of the Kroc Institute survey seem to support the assertion that Pakistan is, in fact, India's principal security concern. For example, 57 percent of those supporting weaponization assert that India should develop nuclear weapons because of a nuclear threat from Pakistan. In addition, 48 percent of those supporting India's current policy viewed a Pakistani nuclear test as a justification for India's development of nuclear weapons. Also, in response to the question of whether India could use nuclear weapons if Pakistan were about to overrun Kashmir, 33 percent of all respondents answered positively.[10] Today India's relations with Pakistan are at their lowest ebb since independence. Despite the existence of formal institutional mechanisms for holding discussions, neither side has shown any great willingness to use them.[11] The Pakistani leadership of Prime Minister Benazir Bhutto has displayed an unusually high degree of intransigence. In late November 1994, the Indian foreign secretary, Krishnan Srinivasan, made an effort to discuss a range of outstanding bilateral issues with his Pakistani counterpart at a meeting of the British Commonwealth Foreign Secretaries in Islamabad, but his Pakistani counterparts firmly rebuffed him.[12]

Assessing Capabilities

Given the realities noted above, any discussion of the prospects for a South Asian nuclear freeze will need to focus on Indian and Pakistani nuclear and ballistic programs. The potential Chinese threat will also have to be considered but at a secondary level. Indian decision makers will continue to fret about China's capabilities and long-term intentions, but these are not perceived as an immediate threat. The findings of the Kroc Institute poll confirm this assessment. Of those who favor the development of nuclear weapons, only 20 percent cite the threat from China as justification, compared to 57 percent who are concerned about a nuclear Pakistan. When other respondents were asked what could justify India's development of nuclear weapons, the prospect of a serious deterioration in relations with China ranked low in priority (only 17 percent among supporters of official policy, compared to 48 percent who cited concern about a possible Pakistani nuclear test). For Indian elites and government decision makers then, the major security concern is indeed Pakistan.

We begin our assessment of the South Asian security equation with a review of India's nuclear capabilities. Currently, India has a dozen nuclear power plants. Eleven of them are on-line as of early 1995. The twelfth, at Kakrapar, has been commissioned but has not yet started operations. Seven of the operating plants are not under IAEA full-scope safeguards. India's two research reactors at Trombay, and its eight heavy water facilities, which operate at varying levels of efficiency, are also outside the IAEA safeguards system.

Thus far, India has conducted only one nuclear test, in 1974. Though dubbed a "peaceful nuclear explosion" (PNE), for all practical purposes it was a public demonstration of India's bomb-making capabilities. The sharp international condemnation of India's actions in the wake of the 1974 test is the most likely reason India's decision makers have not conducted further tests. Three international reactions need to be underscored: the December 1974 Canadian decision to break off nuclear cooperation with India, the creation of the London Nuclear Supplier's Club in 1975, and the passage of the U.S. Nuclear Non-Proliferation Act (NNPA) in 1978. These played a large role in squelching India's nuclear ambition after the 1974 test. The Canadian reaction was particularly sharp. It is widely believed that the plutonium for India's PNE came from the Canadian-supplied Cirus research reactor at Trombay, which was supplied only if it would be used exclusively for peaceful purposes. To avoid future legal problems with Canada, India commissioned the indigenously built 100-megawatt Dhruva reactor, a scaled-up version of the Cirus, from which it now derives plutonium for its weapons program.[13]

Along with its capabilities to produce plutonium from the Dhruva reactor, India has modest uranium 235 enrichment capabilities. Uranium 235 is obtained by irradiating natural, nonradioactive thorium in a reactor.[14] Although India's enrichment facilities are limited, it possesses the world's largest deposits of natural thorium, which are located in the southern state of Kerala. The improvement of these enrichment facilities over time will give India the capability to manufacture bombs out of uranium as well as plutonium.

Finally, India can also manufacture tritium, which can be used to produce tritium-boosted fission weapons. According to one source, small amounts of tritium mixed with equal amounts of deuterium in a warhead can increase severalfold the yield of a fission explosion.[15]

Regarding delivery systems, India currently possesses several squadrons of combat aircraft, including the Soviet-built MiG-27, which can carry nuclear weapons. Moreover, India's Defence Research and Development Organisation (DRDO) has developed the *Agni*, a missile with a payload of between 500 and 1,000 kilograms and a range of 1,600 to 2,500 miles. Additionally, DRDO developed a smaller, short-range missile, the *Prithvi*, which has a range of around 250 kilometers. The *Prithvi* can also be configured to carry nuclear weapons.

In comparison with India's moderately well developed nuclear infrastructure and ballistic missile programs, Pakistan's nuclear and missile capabilities are limited. Pakistan has only one operating nuclear power plant, at Karachi, which uses heavy water and natural uranium. This facility is under the IAEA safeguards system. All three of its uranium enrichment facilities, two of which are currently operating, are outside the realm of safeguards. Furthermore, its four uranium processing plants and three plutonium extraction plants are also without safeguards.

During the 1980s Pakistan received substantial amounts of American economic and military assistance due to its important role in the Afghan War. Under pressure from members of the U.S. Congress interested in nonproliferation, the Reagan administration's allies in the Senate passed the Pressler Amendment to the Foreign Assistance Act, which required the president to certify that Pakistan did not possess a nuclear explosive device before providing assistance. (It did not explicitly prevent Pakistan from continuing work on nuclear weapons development.) As a result, Pakistan gave assurances to the Reagan administration that it would not enrich uranium above 5 percent. It is believed that Pakistan violated this commitment and started to produce weapons-grade uranium (enriched over 90 percent) at its facilities in Kahuta near Islamabad.[16]

Unlike India, however, Pakistan has never tested a nuclear explosive device. Nevertheless, evidence exists that Pakistan has received bomb design assistance from China. Experts on the Pakistani nuclear program also assert that Pakistan has tested the nonnuclear high-explosive triggering devices for a nuclear weapon.[17]

In addition to its nuclear infrastructure, Pakistan has limited nuclear delivery capabilities. For combat aircraft Pakistan uses the U.S.-supplied F-16. With Chinese assistance, it has developed and tested the *Hatf I* and *Hatf II* missiles, with ranges of 80 and 300 kilometers respectively.[18] More recently, press and intelligence reports suggest that it has also acquired and may deploy the Chinese-built M-11 missile.[19]

One problem with assessing the prospects of a South Asian nuclear freeze stems from the opaque character of the nuclear weapons programs of both India and Pakistan, particularly the military aspects of their programs.[20] Nevertheless, the salient features of each country's program are visible and measurable. With a careful analysis of the civilian programs, especially those not under the aegis of full-scope safeguards, one can assess the weapons production capacities of both states. According to one authoritative estimate, India has sufficient plutonium to produce as many as sixty and possibly eighty nuclear weapons. The same source asserts that Pakistan could deploy between fifteen and twenty-five nuclear weapons.[21]

Toward Cold Storage

A small but growing body of literature exists on the prospects of a nuclear freeze in South Asia, although, with one important exception, these analyses address the nuclear freeze question indirectly.[22] Mitchell Reiss contends that if both India and Pakistan could be persuaded to adopt full-scope IAEA safeguards on their nuclear programs, the South Asian nuclear conundrum could be resolved.[23] From technical and legal standpoints his argument is persuasive and sophisticated. A full-scope safeguards regime with the appropriate forms of verification that Reiss envisages would, in effect, amount to a nuclear freeze. However, he fails to adequately address the complex politics of the region. For instance, Reiss reports that Pakistani decision makers would quite promptly agree to sign a full-scope safeguards agreement along with India. This apparent willingness, however, is disingenuous. The Pakistanis are more than well aware that no Indian government would sign such an agreement, because it would not address India's professed misgivings about China. Pakistan is simply trying to embarrass India and seize the high moral ground by adopting what otherwise appears to be a cooperative stance. A full-scope safeguards regime in South Asia, though technically feasible, is little more than a political chimera.

George Perkovich's notion of "non-weaponized deterrence" also assumes some form of a nuclear weapons production freeze. Deterrence, according to this logic, would be based upon latent capabilities rather than deployed weaponry. As Perkovich argues, India and Pakistan ". . . simply seem to accept the basic and mutual deterrent effects of one country's capability to drop a nuclear weapon on the other."[24] Perkovich's argument is clearly on target; a crude form of nuclear stability appears to have arrived on the subcontinent. Neither India nor Pakistan are now prepared to resort to full-scale war despite the sanguinary situation in Kashmir because decision makers on both sides are aware of the nuclear capabilities of the other. In a sense, we are seeing a variant of Glenn Snyder's famous "stability/instability" paradox.[25] Stability at the level of nuclear weapons prevents the outbreak of full-scale war while permitting both sides to engage in low-level conflict.

Perkovich's conception of "non-weaponized deterrence" would differ from the present situation on the subcontinent in three ways. First, both India and Pakistan would refrain from deploying nuclear delivery systems. Second, both sides would agree on what level of nuclear weapons preparation was permissible with appropriate means of verification. Third, time buffers would have to be built into the nuclear weapons complexes to bolster crisis stability and escalation control.

The only shortcoming of Perkovich's analysis is that it fails to address directly Indian concerns about China's expanding nuclear capabilities. Chinese assurances for a no first use pledge, which Perkovich calls for, have little or no resonance in New Delhi. Nor would the removal of Chinese missiles from Tibet amount to much, as the missiles could well be trundled back when the occasion so required. These caveats notwithstanding, Perkovich's analysis is a useful starting point for discussing the prospects of a nuclear freeze on the subcontinent. Moreover, given the diminished perceptions of the Chinese threat mentioned above, it may be more politically feasible now to strike a separate nuclear deal with Islamabad.

Sandy Gordon addresses the issue of a nuclear freeze more directly.[26] Gordon's argument is sensitive to Indian concerns over China's nuclear and ballistic missile capabilities and concedes India's need to maintain a threshold-deterrent capability against China. The crux of his argument lies in India's willingness to join a global UN-sponsored weapons-grade fissile material production cutoff, and India's acquiescence to a comprehensive test ban treaty (CTBT). Gordon recognizes that China is unwilling to be part of a South Asian nuclear freeze process, but might be willing to participate in a global arrangement banning testing and the production of fissile material.

Only unrelenting advocates of a missile technology control regime would find fault with Gordon's otherwise excellent analysis. They would contend that leaving India with its threshold-deterrent capability would provide a carte blanche to India's incipient ballistic missile program. Such an argument, though seemingly compelling, is ultimately facile: Indian elites are not eager to enter a full-fledged ballistic missile race with China. Furthermore, once it attained a threshold capability, India could be induced to enter into various regional arms control agreements.

James Leonard and Adam M. Scheinman advance a thoughtful and imaginative analysis based on the fact that, despite incremental steps, India has not tested a second nuclear device, and that Pakistan, under U.S. and international pressure, has also shown some restraint in its nuclear program.[27] They also recognize that India is unlikely to join the Nuclear Nonproliferation Treaty (NPT), which it sees as fundamentally discriminatory, and that as a result, Pakistan is also unwilling to join the NPT regime. Consequently, the authors contend that it would be best to pursue universal measures such as a comprehensive test ban, a fissile material production cutoff and a no first use agreement.[28] All these measures have some prospect of implementation on the subcontinent because they are within the realm of political feasibility.

A similar set of arguments is advanced in another multiauthored study on preventing proliferation in South Asia.[29] This study, conducted under the auspices of the Asia Society, supports some variant of a nuclear freeze in South Asia. The report builds on Perkovich's concept of "nonweaponized deterrence." It also discusses the tension between the degree of opacity necessary to protect incipient nuclear weapons systems versus the degree of transparency necessary to prevent strategic surprise. However, it does not explicitly spell out the technical conditions under which a freeze would be viable. Such technical issues, the report suggests, are important subjects requiring further research and analysis.

The literature surveyed here suggests possible pathways of shifting from the present Indian and Pakistani positions of nuclear ambiguity. Yet both technical and political hurdles have to be overcome before any shift can take place. To discuss the possibilities of an alternate position it is necessary to recognize that the nuclear situation in South Asia is fraught with many difficulties, all of which could prove destabilizing. These factors include the incremental development of ballistic missiles, the problems associated with command and control, and inadvertent escalation from conventional conflict.

The deployment of ballistic missiles with extraordinarily short warning times, as the literature suggests, could prove to be highly destabilizing in a crisis. Under crisis conditions both sides would have every temptation to strike preemptively. Consequently, the present trend toward the introduction of intermediate-range ballistic missiles needs to be stemmed.

The command and control (C^3I)[30] of existing nuclear forces needs to be strengthened. Organizational and technical measures need to be instituted to ensure that weapons cannot be assembled in a short time. Furthermore, mechanisms have to be devised to prevent the accidental, inadvertent, or unauthorized usage of nuclear weapons.

Finally, the improvement of C^3I would also reduce the likelihood of the inadvertent escalation in case of the outbreak of conventional war. To this end, the relevant decision makers in the political and military establishments in both India and Pakistan need to assess carefully and honestly the crises of 1987 and 1990.

Warming to a Freeze

Despite the seemingly intractable security situation in South Asia, there are reasons for cautious and modest optimism in the arms control arena. Both India and Pakistan have made fitful progress toward the discussion of a fissile material production cutoff under UN auspices.[31] During preliminary discussions within the UN Conference on Disarmament, Pakistan has insisted that negotiations for a fissile material cutoff cover the existing stockpiles of the nuclear powers. Islamabad urged that the proposed agreement include a declaration by the nuclear weapons states of their current stockpiles and the application of safeguards to these materials.[32] India was an original sponsor of the resolution during the United Nations General Assembly of 1993. This resolution was reintroduced on 16 December 1994.[33] India has also cosponsored a UN resolution calling for a comprehensive test ban treaty (CTBT).[34] Pakistan, although not a cosponsor of the CTBT resolution, is nevertheless a supporter of the CTBT process.

The other state directly relevant to these efforts is China. Beijing supports the negotiations on the fissile material production cutoff. Their position on the CTBT is more complex, however. Asserting that they support the CTBT process in principle, they have nevertheless refused to join the testing moratorium and insist that they will conduct nuclear tests until 1996.[35] This Chinese insistence on testing stems from China's plans to modernize its nuclear arsenal.

These fitful supports of a fissile material production cutoff and the CTBT form the key components of a nuclear freeze in the region. They are essential because if enacted in tandem they ensure that the nuclear programs in India, Pakistan, and China will not be able to develop further. But two other elements are essential to making a freeze complete. First, adequate mechanisms must be developed for verifying the production cutoff and test ban. Second, some restraints must be placed on the continued testing and development of ballistic missiles in the region. The ban on testing and fissile material production would involve crossing some technical hurdles but hardly insuperable ones. The political problems with a ban are far more difficult. The question of limiting ballistic missiles in the region, at least in the Indo-Pakistani context, is somewhat less problematic, although India's long-range ballistic missile program, largely seen as a potential deterrent against China, poses a different problem.

How could the cutoff of production of weapons-grade fissile material be verified? Regional experts, particularly from India, have discussed both the political and (ostensible) technical difficulties of ensuring a verifiable cutoff.[36] Unfortunately, most of the arguments advanced are polemical. The technical difficulties that are adduced stem largely from the differences in reactor design and nuclear fuel; most of Pakistan's reactors rely on uranium while Indian reactors are plutonium fueled. Admittedly, these differences complicate a mutual verification process. But they are not insurmountable.

A verifiable cutoff of weapons-grade fissile material would entail two broad categories of controls: one on the production of weapons-grade fissile material, the other on the use of stockpiled material. On the first issue, one authoritative study by Neuhoff and Singer concludes that an upper limit on the possible plutonium rates can be calculated by measuring the output of known reactors. This, in turn, can be determined by using infrared observation from satellites.[37] The monitoring of uranium 235 enrichment facilities of the kind Pakistan possesses, however, apparently gives rise to more complex technical problems and, unlike the less-intrusive methods that may suffice with plutonium reactors, may require more intrusive inspections of centrifuge enrichment areas.[38] This, of course, would be not only a technical but also a political problem.

The assessment of stockpiles presents a greater difficulty. Apparently there exists no simple, nonintrusive technical means for assessing stockpiles of nuclear materials. According to Neuhoff and Singer:

> India and Pakistan face a significant dilemma. Either (1) they must accept unprecedented extensive surveys and mutually imposed controls over fissile materials stockpiles or less extensive assurances with considerable potential uncertainty, or (2) they agree to disparate levels of stockpiled materials under similar constraints, or (3) they enter into very difficult negotiations concerning an approach to acceptable higher levels of fissile materials stockpiles.[39]

The technical difficulties of dealing with existing stockpiles obviously lead to a political problem. The degree of intrusiveness that is necessary for verifying existing stockpiles is simply impossible in the present political context. Political contexts, of course, are not permanent, nor are they unamenable to skillful diplomacy. Nevertheless, they remain extremely important and do limit the possibilities of action.

What about the issue of delivery vehicles? Both India and Pakistan currently possess short-range ballistic missiles. The Indian *Prithvi* has a range sufficient to strike virtually any target within Pakistan. The accuracy of the *Prithvi* remains classified. Pakistan's M-11 missiles, obtained from China, can strike most of India's northwestern airfields and other military targets. In the context of a nuclear freeze, both sides could refrain from deploying the two missiles. Such a ban could be verified through satellite reconnaissance. The drawback, however, is that the United States is perhaps the only state that possesses the required satellite reconnaissance capabilities.[40] In the present political context, it is unclear whether either India or Pakistan would see the United States as a neutral source of information or as a dispassionate observer.

India's pursuit of long-range missile capabilities poses problems of a markedly different order. There is little question that India's development of the *Agni* stems from its perceived necessity to have a viable deterrent against China. Yet this missile can also strike Pakistan with impunity. From a Pakistani standpoint, India's pursuit of the *Agni*, even if supposedly directed at China, is a potential threat. Nonetheless, if India were to enter a fissile material cutoff regime and sign a comprehensive test ban, its ability to weaponize the *Agni* would be severely hobbled. This might not completely assuage Pakistani fears, but it could address them up to a point.

Public Opinion and the Freeze

The findings of the Kroc Institute survey do not suggest overwhelming support for a freeze. No single question specifically addressed the proposal for a nuclear freeze, but attitudes on the issue can be implied from other questions that have bearing on the subject.

Of the 992 individuals polled, a considerable portion can be considered among the likely supporters of a freeze policy. Eight percent believed that India should renounce nuclear weapons under the present circumstances, and another 57 percent held that India should maintain its present posture. Although the present posture may hardly amount to a freeze, it has important elements of restraint: India has not tested a second nuclear device, and has consistently supported both the CTBT and the fissile material production cutoff. It also has yet to deploy the *Prithvi* despite Pakistan's acquisition of the M-11. Consequently, the significant support for the existing policy could be interpreted as support for some level of nuclear restraint. To the extent that New Delhi has given diplomatic support to key elements of a freeze, the broad public endorsement of official policy could be interpreted as a form of indirect support for a freeze.

The responses to other questions also lend support to a freeze. A total of 326 respondents, one-third of the sample, expressed support for outright weaponization. When this group was asked what circumstances would permit India to renounce nuclear weapons, 42 percent identified the prospect of a "time-bound plan for global disarmament." From this finding one can imply strong support for the pursuit of universal measures to reduce and eliminate nuclear weapons. Since the components of a freeze (test ban, fissile material cutoff, and comprehensive safeguards) point in this direction, this finding suggests a further base of potential support. A further set of questions to nuclear advocates also elicited hopeful responses. When this group was asked how far India should go in developing nuclear weapons, 34 percent held that India should "develop all components but not actually assemble any nuclear weapon." In itself this position does not constitute a nuclear freeze. However, the option would approach the characteristics of a freeze if it could be coupled with a commitment to greater transparency. In any case it reflects a preference for restraint that would be consistent with a freeze policy.

The sheer technical complexity of the subject and the paucity of information and public debate on the subject of nuclear weapons makes it difficult to judge with much confidence the extent of public support for a nuclear freeze. Additionally, the "epistemic community" in South Asia dealing with the question of nuclear weapons remains exceedingly small.[41] Only a few scholars and journalists have challenged the "hegemonic discourse" that characterizes the nuclear weapons question.[42] Even many of these critics remain opposed to India's accession to the NPT owing to its discriminatory character. But surveys of urban elites made by the U.S. Information Agency (USIA) suggest that there is a considerable base of support for at least a conditional nuclear freeze among this select, but influential, population. For instance, a poll conducted by the USIA in April of 1994 found that 84 percent of a sample of 830 college graduates agreed that India, Pakistan, and China should all agree to freeze the nuclear arms race in the region.[43] But within this group a majority (63 percent) rejected the possibility of a unilateral freeze.[44] These data, combined with the results of the Kroc Institute survey and other USIA data, suggest that any steps toward a freeze must be taken in a transparent, multilateral context if they are to sustain popular support.

Given the state of the nuclear debate within India it appears that the freeze option can best be addressed through multilateral and nondiscriminatory measures. Consequently, to prepare the ground for greater transparency it is imperative that progress is made toward a global fissile material cutoff regime and a CTBT. Short of these "good faith" actions by the nuclear weapons states, little movement will take place in either India or Pakistan toward a freeze.

India's continued pursuit of a ballistic missile program also poses a problem for a nuclear freeze regime in South Asia. As argued earlier, the missile program is designed to ward off a potential Chinese threat. However, vigorous pursuit of the missile program may well bring about the very situation that India fears most, namely, Chinese targeting of incipient Indian missile capabilities. Thus far, China has shown scant interest in addressing India's misgivings about the Chinese nuclear threat. Nevertheless, it may behoove Indian decision makers, who have dealt with the Chinese conventional threat with some dexterity, to now turn their attention to some form of regional arms control that includes China.[45]

Shifting the terms of debate within South Asia will be a daunting task. Public opinion offers some evidence for indirect support of a freeze, but the poll results also show support for outright development of nuclear weapons. Building support for a freeze will require skillful diplomacy internationally and enlightened political leadership at home. The task is difficult but not impossible. Incremental steps toward denuclearization are critical before the nuclear weapons programs in the region can be effectively placed in cold storage.

Notes

1. An important and thoughtful exception remains Bhabani Sen Gupta, ed., *Nuclear Weapons? Policy Options for India* (New Delhi: Sage, 1983).

2. For a description and analysis of the three Indo-Pakistani conflicts see Sumit Ganguly, *The Origins of War in South Asia: The Indo-Pakistani Conflicts Since 1947* (Boulder, Colo.: Westview, 1994). The best analysis of the origins of the Sino-Indian border conflict is Steven Hoffmann's *India and the China Crisis* (Berkeley, Calif.: The Univ. of California Press, 1990).

3. Kanti Bajpai, P.R. Chari, Pervaiz Iqbal Cheema, Stephen P. Cohen, and Sumit Ganguly, *Brasstacks and Beyond: Perception and Management of Crisis in South Asia* (Urbana, Ill.: Program in Arms Control, Disarmament and International Security, 1995).

4. A description and assessment of this crisis can be found in Seymour Hersh, "On the Nuclear Edge," *The New Yorker*, 29 March 1993.

5. Sumit Ganguly, *Slouching Towards a Settlement: Sino-Indian Relations, 1962–1993*, Asia Program Monograph No. 60 (Washington, D.C.: The Woodrow Wilson International Center for Scholars, 1990).

6. Lena H. Sun, "China, India Sign Accord To Ease Border Dispute," *The Washington Post*, 8 September 1993.

7. Ganguly, *Slouching Towards a Settlement*.

8. See Mya Muang, "On the Road to Mandalay: A Case Study of the Sinoization of Upper Burma," *Asian Survey* 34, no. 5 (May 1994): 447–59. Also see Ross H. Munro, "The Asian Interior: China's Waxing Spheres of Influence," *Orbis* 38, no. 4 (Fall 1994): 585–605.

9. For a thorough discussion of the international constraints, especially the Missile Technology Control Regime, see Brahma Chellaney, *Nuclear Proliferation: The U.S.-Indian Conflict* (New Delhi: Orient Longman, 1993).

10. The frequency of this response to the question When could India use nuclear weapons? was second only to never, which was selected by 44 percent of all respondents.

11. See John Sandrock and Michael Maldony, *The History and Future of Confidence Building Measures in South Asia: A Background Paper* (McLean, Va.: Science Applications International Corporation [SAIC], 1994).

12. Tarun Basu and Tariq Butt, "Pakistan Says 'No' to Attempt at Dialogue," *India Abroad* 25, no. 9 (2 December 1994): 14.

13. David Albright and Mark Hibbs, "India's Silent Bomb," *The Bulletin of the Atomic Scientists* 48, no. 7 (September 1992): 27–31.

14. Ibid., 29.

15. Ibid., 30.

16. David Albright and Tom Zamora, "India, Pakistan's Nuclear Weapons: All the Pieces in Place," *The Bulletin of the Atomic Scientists* 45, no. 5 (June 1989): 20–26.

17. Ibid., 21–22.

18. George Perkovich, "A Nuclear Third Way in South Asia," *Foreign Policy*, no. 91 (Summer 1993): 85–104.

19. Steven A. Holmes, "China Denies Violating Pact By Selling Arms to Pakistan," *The New York Times*, 26 July 1993, A2.

20. On the issue of "opaque" nuclear proliferation see Benjamin Frankel, ed., *Opaque Nuclear Proliferation* (London: Frank Cass, 1991). For a thoughtful application of the concept to the South Asian context see Devin T. Hagerty, "The Power of

Suggestion: Opaque Proliferation, Existential Deterrence, and the South Asian Nuclear Competition," *Security Studies* 2, nos. 3/4 (Spring/Summer 1993).

21. Personal communication with Leonard Spector, director, Nonproliferation Project, The Carnegie Endowment for International Peace, Washington, D.C.

22. See for example, Mitchell Reiss, "Safeguarding the Nuclear Peace in South Asia," *Asian Survey* 33, no. 12 (December 1993): 1107–21; and George Perkovich, "A Nuclear Third Way in South Asia." The key exception is Sandy Gordon, "Capping South Asia's Nuclear Weapons Programs: A Window of Opportunity?" *Asian Survey* 34, no. 7 (July 1994): 662–73.

23. Reiss, "Safeguarding," 1113–20.

24. Perkovich, "A Nuclear Third Way," 88.

25. Glenn Snyder, *Deterrence and Defense* (Westport Conn.: Greenwood, 1975).

26. Gordon, "Capping South Asia's Nuclear Weapons Programs."

27. James F. Leonard and Adam M. Scheinman, "Denuclearizing South Asia: Global Approaches to a Regional Problem," *Arms Control Today* 23, no. 5 (June 1993): 17–22.

28. Ibid., 17.

29. Marshall Bouton, et al., *Preventing Proliferation in South Asia: The Report of a Study Group* (New York, N.Y.: The Asia Society, 1994).

30. Command, control, communications, and intelligence.

31. Discussions with two ACDA officials, 15 December, 1994. The Pakistani willingness to join the UN-sponsored discussions of a fissile material production cutoff was hinged on their concerns about previous stockpiles of nuclear material. Only after their misgivings were suitably assuaged did they agree in early December 1994 to the UN "negotiating mandate."

32. Tom Zamora Collina, "Cutoff Talks Delayed," *The Bulletin of the Atomic Scientists* 51, no. 2 (March/April 1995): 16.

33. This draft resolution calls on the UN Conference on Disarmament to: ". . . complete negotiations at the earliest date for an appropriate mandate for the Ad Hoc Committee on a non-discriminatory, multilateral and internationally and effectively verifiable treaty banning the production of fissile material for nuclear weapons or other nuclear explosive devices. . . ." UN Consensus Resolution 48/75L, 16 December 1994.

34. Resolution 48/70 introduced 16 December 1993 at the United Nations General Assembly, New York.

35. Discussions with ACDA official, 15 December 1994.

36. R.R. Subramaniam and K. Subrahmanyam, "Mutual Inspection and Verification," in *India and the Nuclear Challenge,* ed. K. Subrahmanyam (New Delhi: Lancers, 1986). It is pertinent to note that those opposed to a nuclear freeze in the superpower context also raised similar objections about verifiability. A good discussion of the ramifications of a nuclear freeze in the context of U.S./Soviet relations can be found in Paul M. Cole and William J. Taylor, Jr., eds., *The Nuclear Freeze Debate: Arms Control Issues for the 1980s* (Boulder, Colo.: Westview, 1983).

37. Jon Neuhoff and Clifford Singer, "Verification and Control of Fissile Materials," in *Nuclear Proliferation in South Asia: The Prospects for Arms Control*, ed. Stephen P. Cohen (Boulder, Colo.: Westview, 1991).

38. Ibid., 217.

39. Ibid., 218–19.

40. This is also subject to change in the foreseeable future. Though the political imperatives may not yet exist, Japan is rapidly acquiring the requisite capabilities to monitor arms control agreements in the region. See Bhupendra Jasani and Toshibomi Sakata, eds., *Satellites for Arms Control and Crisis Monitoring* (Oxford: SIPRI/Oxford Univ. Press, 1987).

41. The concept of an "epistemic community" is discussed in Peter Haas, "Introduction: Epistemic Communities and International Policy Coordination," *International Organization* 46, no. 1 (Winter 1992): 1–35.

42. The concept of "hegemonic discourse" is derived from Antonio Gramsci. See Benedetto Fontana, *Hegemony and Power: On the Relationship Between Gramsci and Machiavelli* (Minneapolis: Univ. of Minnesota Press, 1993). One of the rare critiques of the Indian nuclear weapons program is Praful Bidwai and Achin Vanaik, "India and Pakistan," in *Security With Nuclear Weapons?* ed. Regina Cowen Karp (Oxford: SIPRI/Oxford Univ. Press, 1991). Also see Achin Vanaik, "Political Case for a NWFZ in South Asia," *Economic and Political Weekly* 10, no. 48 (30 November 1985): 2115–20. For an early but idiosyncratic critique see Dhirendra Sharma, *India's Nuclear Estate* (New Delhi: Lancers, 1983). For a Pakistani critique of nuclear weapons on the subcontinent see M.B. Naqvi, "The Nuclear Mirage," *Newsline*, April 1994, 34b–38.

43. Elaine El Assal, "Indian Elites Support Three-Way Regional Nuclear Freeze But Reject Unilateral Cap," M-128-94, United States Information Agency *Opinion Research Memorandum*, 27 May 1994, 6.

44. Ibid., 7.

45. This, of course, will not be easy. For a thoughtful discussion of emergent Chinese strategic interests in Asia see David Shambaugh, "Growing Strong: China's Challenge to Asian Security," *Survival* 36, no. 2 (Summer 1994): 43–59.

5

Going Nuclear: Establishing an Overt Nuclear Weapons Capability

Varun Sahni

For the proponents of an Indian nuclear deterrent, the term "going nuclear" has an almost mythical resonance. Shorn of its symbolic and rhetorical superstructure and seen in a cold, analytical light, this term merely indicates the crossing of a line. A country is said to have "gone nuclear" when it declares that it has developed and deployed nuclear weapons. *Development*, *deployment*, and *declaration* are the three essential elements of the policy option called "going nuclear."

The line between going nuclear and not doing so is depicted in academic and policy literature alike as a nuclear Rubicon, an atomic *Lakshmana Rekha*.[1] Despite some notable instances of nuclear "rollback" in recent years, such as the shutting down of the South African nuclear weapons program,[2] the "point of no return" remains a basic notion in the debate about proliferation in South Asia.

While nuclear policy must be subjected to systematic and rational inquiry, the dreams (and nightmares) that adhere to all things nuclear must be factored into our analysis. Not to do so would be to ignore an important element in the decision of national leadership to build the bomb. Nuclear history is replete with its Italian navigators and Smiling Buddhas,[3] with dreams of national muscularity and fears of national emasculation and extinction. From the very beginning, relations between the human being and the nuclear genie have been a fable of fear and temptation.

The nonrational may be intangible, but it is nonetheless both perceptible and real. Therefore, alone among the various nuclear choices analyzed in this volume, the option of going nuclear has to contend not only with matters of the head but also with matters of the heart. Both the head and the heart are very evident when we examine the reasons advanced by the supporters of India's nuclear weapons option. As suggested in the classical literature, the motivations are essentially those of *security* and *prestige*. The security motivation is based on the notion of "nuclear asymmetry," the central argument being that a country cannot be successfully defended by conventional forces against an adversary with nuclear forces.[4] In terms of the basic battlefield tactics of *concentration* and *dispersal* of forces, an army facing a situation of nuclear asymmetry would be unable to concentrate its forces where they are needed for fear of losing them in a nuclear attack, while the nuclear-armed adversary would face no such limitation. The advocates of India going nuclear therefore regard the national security threat arising from a situation of nuclear asymmetry as intolerable. The basic proposition on which they base their analysis is that only nuclear weapons can deter nuclear weapons.

In the eyes of the nuclear proponents, the security argument for going nuclear is further bolstered by the fact that Pakistan and China, the two countries with which India has fought four wars between 1947 and 1971, are respectively a threshold nuclear power and a declared nuclear weapons state. Let us first consider the Pakistani case, which looms large for Indian policymakers, opinion shapers, and analysts. The Kroc Institute poll shows that most of those who support a pronuclear stance viewed threats from a nuclear Pakistan as the main justification for India's nuclear weapons production. The various pieces of the Pakistani nuclear jigsaw puzzle have slowly been coming together over the last decade. Many pieces of the puzzle still need to be filled, but the essential picture must surely be clear by now to all but the most visually challenged and imagination deficient. We can briefly summarize what we know. Ever since the 1971 war and the creation of Bangladesh by the Indian armed forces, successive Pakistani military and civilian governments have, with ingenuity and single-minded devotion, pursued a nuclear program that is clandestine, tightly controlled, military in its organization and intentions, reasonably successful in its outcomes, and hugely popular within the country. As Zulfikar Bhutto, later president of Pakistan, declared in 1965, "if India builds the bomb, we will eat grass to get one of our own."[5] On 23 August 1994, former Pakistani prime minister Nawaz Sharif unequivocally declared in a public meeting that "Pakistan possesses the atom bomb."[6] It is extremely significant that three days later, Sharif's bitter political rival, Prime Minister Benazir Bhutto, did not refute his statement but merely called it "irresponsible."[7]

Pakistan's nuclear weapons program was conceived neither for reasons of prestige nor in pursuit of the mythical Islamic bomb,[8] as has been suggested by some analysts in the West, but for concrete security reasons after military defeat and geographical dismemberment by India, a country which many Pakistanis consider an implacable foe. This distinction is very important, because it means that a Pakistani nuclear arsenal would be deployed solely against India, Pakistan's only real security threat. Most Indian policymakers view the prospect of a nuclear Pakistan with considerable unease; some even suggest it as the ultimate security nightmare for India. General K. Sundarji, former chief of the Indian army, has suggested two broad warfighting scenarios in which a nuclear Pakistan could launch a first strike against India.[9] Both these scenarios involve either forestalling or blunting a conventional Indian counteroffensive into Pakistan in the plains of eastern Punjab. Thus, the historical maneuver resorted to by India in response to Pakistani aggressive behavior in Kashmir could be denied to it by a nuclear Pakistan.

The security threat posed by China is far less tangible, the 1962 border war notwithstanding. Even in the disputed Himalayan reaches, Chinese behavior toward India has generally been moderate and restrained. Furthermore, there has not been a single instance of "nuclear blackmail" by China, even during the period when China/India relations were particularly estranged. This is reflected in Indian elite opinion. The Kroc Institute poll shows that only 20 percent of the pro-bomb respondents suggested threats from China as a reason to go nuclear.

While China has been scrupulously observant of its no first use nuclear pledge, many Indian analysts are clearly skeptical about its validity. They point to China's program of upgrading and modernizing its strategic arsenal, its creation of a nuclear war fighting capability with the development of tactical nuclear weapons, and its deployment of short-range nuclear weapons in forward areas.[10] In terms of capabilities, Chinese missiles in Xinkiang and Tibet, which are currently targeted at Russia, could be reprogrammed in a matter of minutes onto targets in India. Indian security officials have always been uncomfortable living with the Chinese bomb and at the mercy of Chinese good will.

It has also been pointed out that the end of the cold war *increases* India's vulnerability to Chinese nuclear threats because there is no longer any guarantee that either the U.S. or Russia, the only powers that could apply countervailing nuclear pressure on China, will come to India's aid during a crisis.[11] With the Indo-Soviet Treaty of Peace, Friendship, and Cooperation now consigned to the history books, Russia is far less likely to provide India with a nuclear umbrella against China. The United States was never likely to apply countervailing nuclear pressure on China, even during the darkest days of the cold war, and it is almost inconceivable that this would be the case today. The U.S. has lately shown a marked tendency to bend backwards to avoid alienating China.

Apart from Pakistan and China, other situations of nuclear asymmetry have also been visualized. In particular, some analysts have suggested that the extraregional powers (particularly the U.S. and France) who have deployed ship-based nuclear weapons in the Indian Ocean pose a potential nuclear threat to India.[12] This scenario is not taken very seriously, however. In the Kroc Institute poll, threats from nuclear powers other than Pakistan were suggested as a reason for going nuclear by only 27 percent of the pro-bomb respondents. Therefore, nuclear asymmetry vis-à-vis Pakistan and China presents the predominant security concern for the advocates of an Indian nuclear deterrent.

The other big motivation for going nuclear relates not to national security but to national prestige. This vision is encapsulated in the phrase "currency of power" which was first articulated by K. Subrahmanyam, former secretary of defence [production] and India's most prominent nuclear advocate. The irony here is that Subrahmanyam has now pronounced that "[t]he world in which nuclear weapons could be used as currency of power is gone forever."[13] Nevertheless, many supporters of an Indian nuclear capability, who are only marginally aware of the intricacies of nuclear doctrine, continue to perceive a close relationship between great power status and the bomb. As was mentioned in previous chapters, 49 percent of the pro-bomb respondents in the Kroc Institute poll felt that India should go nuclear to improve its bargaining power in world affairs, while 38 percent of the same group felt that an Indian nuclear arsenal would enhance India's international status.

One of the reasons why some proponents of an Indian nuclear capability perceive a connection between great-power status and the bomb is the correlation that exists among the five veto-wielding permanent members of the United Nations Security Council and the five declared nuclear weapons states (NWS) in the Nuclear Nonproliferation Treaty (NPT). It is not often recalled that permanent membership of the UN Security Council was granted to the Big Five victors of the Second World War and has nothing to do with their *subsequent* nuclear status. Only 14 percent of the pro-bomb respondents felt that India could renounce nuclear weapons in return for a permanent seat on the UN Security Council.

Another motivation for going nuclear is the prestige that technological prowess garners in the modern world. As India gropes its way toward modern nationhood, which implies a modern state *and* a modern society, the bomb can easily become a proud and seductive symbol of national achievement. For many in the developing world, nuclear power is considered the epitome of high technology, the ultimate example of scientific sophistication and advancement. Although the United States and other developed countries are finding that the presumed economic and technological benefits of nuclear power are less than originally assumed, such perceptions have not spread widely yet in India and other developing nations. Especially among elites, nuclear technology still holds the promise of scientific advancement and international prestige.

Who are these supporters, advocates, and proponents of an Indian bomb? In the political arena, the parties on the right of the ideological spectrum have traditionally projected a solidly pro-bomb stance. The party of Hindu assertion and chauvinism, the Bharatiya Janata Party (BJP), has consistently advocated a pronuclear position. Murli Manohar Joshi, former president of the BJP, has often said that India should make the bomb, although Lal Kishan Advani, the present BJP chief, has been more discrete about the party's nuclear stance. The pro-bomb leanings of BJP members are evident from the findings of the Kroc Institute poll. Eighteen percent of the 326 pro-bomb advocates identified in the survey were BJP supporters, while only 11 percent of the supporters of government policy and 5 percent of nuclear opponents identified themselves with the BJP. It is not unheard of for BJP supporters to claim that the *Brahmastra*[14] of the Great Epics, the *Ramayana* and the *Mahabharata*, were primordial nuclear weapons and that a nuclear India would merely be reclaiming its spiritual and technological heritage.

Despite a widespread belief that the Indian armed forces favor establishing a nuclear capability, most military officers do not appear to be particularly pronuclear. In January 1971, eleven months *before* war broke out between India and Pakistan, General J.N. Chaudhury, one of India's most distinguished army chiefs, delivered the inaugural National Security Lecture of the United Service Institution of India, the premier "intellectual club" within the Indian armed forces. In his lecture General Chaudhury expressed distinct skepticism about the contention that nuclear weapons would allow India to "talk from strength."[15] Within the in-house journals of the armed forces one does come across frequent articles that espouse a pro-bomb position,[16] but it would be incorrect to infer that these writings represent an institutional perspective. Skepticism persists within the armed forces primarily because of doubts about the military utility of the bomb. The Kroc Institute poll shows that members of the armed forces and the police are not overwhelmingly in favor of going nuclear. In fact, military and police officers were less likely to favor the development of nuclear weapons than were other professional groups. Thirty percent of the armed forces/police group were nuclear advocates, compared to 41 percent among business executives and 39 percent among lawyers. Among the various occupation groups surveyed in the opinion poll, only diplomats (25 percent) and journalists (29 percent) showed a lesser advocacy of going nuclear. From the military perspective, there are three good reasons why nuclear weapons would be objectionable: they are not usable in military combat, they increase civilian control over the military machine during times of war, and they reduce the money available for conventional weaponry.

From the author's informal conversations with scientists, it would appear that at least some members of India's science and technology community, particularly in experimental disciplines such as particle physics, probably support weaponization of India's nuclear option. Homi J. Bhabha, the father of India's civilian nuclear program, was clearly the most prominent scientist/administrator to be vocal on this issue. In a 1964 memorandum to Prime Minister Jawaharlal Nehru, Bhabha suggested that apart from building power plants and generating electricity, India's nuclear program could also be oriented toward military purposes.[17] Bhabha's successors have been far more circumspect than he in making public their views about a possible Indian nuclear capability. For instance, in his January 1979 presidential address to the Indian National Science Academy, Raja Ramanna, then chairman of the Atomic Energy Commission, said only that "they [atomic weapons] form a class of ultimate weapons of destruction."[18] It is not easy to gauge the extent of support for going nuclear among Indian scientists, but some support certainly does exist among those involved in reactor design and isotope separation. In the Kroc Institute poll, the category defined as "academic/science" showed a slightly greater than average level of support for going nuclear, 36 percent versus 33 percent. But the lack of precision regarding the composition of this category makes it hard to generalize about the attitudes among all scientists. Learning the extent of scientist support for the nuclear option is made more difficult by a bureaucratic culture within technical institutes that frowns on the expression of political opinions. Although scientists in India's nuclear establishments are not bound by the Official Secrets Act (unlike their British counterparts), in practice any scientist who is vocal about this issue risks losing his/her job.

Perhaps the most important and almost certainly the most influential proponents of going nuclear are the analysts and scholars who comprise India's strategic studies fraternity. Scholars such as K. Subrahmanyam, widely regarded as the dean of Indian strategic thinkers, and institutions such as the government-funded but autonomous Institute of Defence Studies and Analyses (IDSA), stand out in this context and can be justly regarded as the keepers of the nuclear flame in India.

Variants of the Nuclear Option

Clearly the choice to go nuclear, like all the other security options available to India, comes with its attendant benefits, costs, and risks. While some of these are basic to the choice itself, others will depend on the level at which India goes nuclear. To attempt a cost/benefit analysis of establishing a nuclear deterrent, it is therefore important to study the various possible nuclear capabilities available to India.

In essence, there are *four* nuclear capability options, ranging from the modest proposal of developing nuclear warheads and delivery systems but not mating them, all the way up to building an intercontinental ballistic missile (ICBM) force capable of striking the Western Hemisphere. The four nuclear capabilities (or postures) may be termed *nonweaponized, minimal, triad,* and *all horizons*.[19] Each has different implications in terms of weapons capability and nuclear doctrine.

Nonweaponized

The idea of a nonweaponized nuclear posture has been articulated and given respectability by George Perkovich.[20] In essence, this posture is built around keeping nuclear warheads separate from delivery systems. Nonmating of warheads with delivery vehicles significantly lengthens the strategic warning time available to nuclear adversaries because the process of transportation, assembly, and deployment of weapons kept at a nonweaponized capability level is necessarily time-consuming. The increased warning time associated with this approach gives the two adversaries, and interested third parties, an opportunity to initiate conflict-resolution measures. Of the pronuclear respondents in the Kroc Institute poll, 34 percent favored the option of developing all the components but not actually assembling any nuclear weapon, which can be interpreted as support for the nonweaponized approach.

A nonweaponized posture can be compared to being just a screwdriver turn away from weaponization. There is one very significant difference in the nonweaponized approach, however. While the "screwdriver turn" option is *ipso facto* covert, the nonweaponized approach is necessarily transparent. For a nonweaponized nuclear regime to work, it must be *verifiable*.

Devising a verification regime for a nonweaponized nuclear capability is difficult but not impossible. Since the production and disposition of fissile material is permissible in a nonweaponized capability, the inspection of nuclear components and warhead cores, an inherently intrusive process, is not necessary. Instead, delivery vehicles can be monitored by using a reliable array of sensors and tags. In particular, it can be ensured that warheads are kept away from delivery systems by careful monitoring of the perimeters and portals of aircraft bases, missile storage facilities, and artillery and missile production facilities. Any sign of radioactivity in these facilities could then be taken to indicate that nuclear warheads are on the same location as delivery systems, thereby leading to precautionary countermeasures by the other side.

A nonweaponized nuclear capability is certainly feasible for India, but this option is viable only if it is adopted in an overt agreement with Pakistan. General Sundarji has stated in a recent article:

> Minimum nuclear deterrence in South Asia can be made to stick without weaponization or deployment in the classic sense, provided certain tacit understandings are arrived at regarding the continued maintenance of capped but live capabilities of weaponizing at short notice and having the requisite delivery means, but not marrying them with warheads and deploying them in advance.[21]

Although Sundarji mentions capping (i.e., freezing the nuclear weapons program, and particularly the production of fissile materials, at current levels) it is important to emphasize that capping is *not* an essential element of a nonweaponized nuclear capability. In other words, it would not be improper for a country in a nonweaponized regime to persist in its production of fissile material, warhead cores, and delivery vehicles, *as long as it does not mate warhead with delivery system*. Nonetheless, without some sort of capping of capabilities, a nonweaponized regime is unlikely to be stable for long.

A major problem with this option is that China is missing from the equation. This is, of course, a major obstacle, since China has long figured in India's strategic calculations. Because of this limitation, an India/Pakistan nuclear deal would by itself be insufficient.

Minimal

The clearest statement of what a minimal nuclear capability for India would look like has been made by K. Subrahmanyam.[22] He suggests that a small nuclear force does not require an elaborate doctrinal architecture to sustain its credibility. As long as a nuclear capability is aimed only at deterrence (i.e., threatening unacceptable damage on the attacker) and not at actually fighting a nuclear war, a very simple deployment pattern, an uncomplicated targeting philosophy, and a relatively primitive command, control, communications, and intelligence (C^3I) system will suffice.

Since it is not aimed at nuclear warfare, a minimal nuclear capability would focus on countervalue rather than counterforce targets. In other words, the weapons would be aimed on the adversary's population centers (cities) rather than its nuclear facilities (missile silos, submarine pens, and air bases). This approach would have two advantages, according to strategic planners. The possibility of a substantial loss of population will deter an adversary more than the loss of a substantial portion of its nuclear arsenal. Secondly, delivery systems could be far less accurate, and nuclear warheads far less powerful, against "soft" targets such as cities than those used to strike "hard" targets such as missile silos. Subrahmanyam advocates a nuclear force consisting of sixty standard 125 kiloton warheads. Twenty of these warheads could be mounted on MiG and Mirage aircraft, combined with twenty *Prithvi* short-range ballistic missiles (SRBMs)[23] and twenty *Agni* intermediate-range ballistic missiles (IRBMs).[24]

Furthermore, an elaborate C^{3}I system is unnecessary for a minimal nuclear capability, since the nuclear weapons crews would have been instructed to launch according to standard operating procedure. Thus, if attacked by nuclear weapons, India would respond not in a matter of minutes, as with "launch on warning" procedures, but in hours or even days. This still leaves open the question of "use or lose," namely the possibility that a large-scale first strike by a nuclear adversary could destroy the small Indian nuclear deterrent. Subrahmanyam does not consider this a realistic scenario with Pakistan or China, the two most likely nuclear adversaries. While Pakistan faces "technological and resource limitations" that will prevent it from building a large arsenal, China would be loath to use its ICBMs, which it needs as a deterrent against the U.S. and Russia, in a large-scale first strike against India. Thus, the limitation of the size of the adversary's first strike "enhances the survival probability" of the Indian nuclear deterrent at a minimal capability level.[25]

How would Pakistan react to an Indian minimal nuclear capability? Subrahmanyam regards the establishment of a Pakistani minimal deterrent as perfectly acceptable, and suggests that twenty nuclear weapons on its nuclear-capable aircraft would be more than sufficient to deter India. Indeed, if one accepts Subrahmanyam's reasoning, such a Pakistani capability may even be positively desirable, since it would stabilize the India/Pakistan military equation, and eventually could even lead to substantial cuts in the conventional forces of both countries.

Subrahmanyam advocates a minimal capability against China purely for neutralizing Chinese possibilities for nuclear blackmail. Since China is a weaker nuclear power than the U.S. and Russia, it does not have an incentive to legitimize the use of nuclear weapons. Thus, a large-scale Chinese first strike against Indian targets is highly unlikely. As noted earlier, China has only a limited number of ICBMs, and the possibility of their use against India is low. A small retaliatory nuclear force of the minimal-capability level would therefore be sufficient for the purposes of deterrence against both China and Pakistan.

Triad

The establishment of a triad nuclear capability involves reproducing, even if in miniature, the organizational structure and doctrinal architecture of U.S. and Russian strategic forces built during the classic period of superpower confrontation. With India, it would involve the building of a nuclear force similar in many ways to the British, French, and Chinese nuclear forces.

What is meant by nuclear triad? In essence, it implies a strategic nuclear force that has delivery capabilities that are simultaneously based on land, at sea, and in the air, each leg of the triad having its own particular logic of existence and utility. Historically, aerial delivery systems were the first to be developed, as personneled bomber aircraft and the doctrine of strategic bombing, both of which were important parts of the Second World War. The biggest disadvantage of the personneled bomber is that, unlike the delivery systems that comprise the other two legs of the triad, it is *personneled*. That, however, is also its biggest advantage, since it is the only leg of the triad that can be recalled after a launch. Land-based delivery systems such as SRBMs, IRBMs, and ICBMs were the next to be developed, using in no small measure the skills and experience gained by German rocket technology during the Second World War. They are the least expensive leg of the triad, but also the most vulnerable to a first strike by the adversary. The final leg of the triad is based at sea, and consists of nuclear-propelled fleet ballistic missile submarines (SSBNs) armed with submarine-launched ballistic missiles (SLBMs). Easily the most expensive leg of the nuclear triad, this component is also the most secure from a preemptive attack. Since nuclear-powered submarines are mobile, and can remain submerged for months, they are virtually invulnerable. Therefore, they are the most appropriate delivery system for an assured second strike capability.

The most comprehensive study of a triad nuclear capability for India is by Brigadier Vijai K. Nair.[26] He suggests a nuclear force consisting of 132 nuclear warheads of four different yields—1 megaton, 200–500 kilotons, 20–50 kilotons, and 15 kilotons. The sea leg of the triad would consist of five SSBNs, three for deterrence requirements against China (two on patrol, one in reserve), and two against Pakistan (one each on patrol and in reserve). While each of the SSBNs would carry sixteen SLBMs, the entire SLBM inventory (including reserves) would consist of eighty missiles. The land-based delivery systems would comprise twelve *Prithvi* SRBMs and thirty-six *Agni* IRBMs, all aimed at counterforce targets. The air leg would consist of the combat aircraft already in the Indian inventory, and would have an exclusively countervalue role. Given the proximity of the adversaries (Pakistan and China) to India, a reliable, survivable, and flexible C³I system that operates in real time is essential. Nair proposes the establishment of two "national command centers" and eight "military command centers" throughout the country for C³I purposes. Clearly, the establishment of a triad capability of this sort raises a number of questions of cost and feasibility. These will be analyzed later in the chapter.

Given its inherent complexity, a triad nuclear capability also requires a coherent nuclear strategy with the appropriate doctrinal architecture. This would consist of a clearly enunciated and credible declaratory policy, a rational employment and targeting policy, and an optimal deployment policy. However, in order for this doctrinal architecture to be credible, doctrine would have to be matched by capability. Thus, the range, accuracy, payload, force levels, safeguards, and C^3I of the warheads and delivery vehicles must buttress the nuclear doctrine.

Nair also suggests an elaborate targeting schedule. Six cities including a port, one battlefield target (corps sized offensive formation in its concentration area), two dams, five military airfields, and three strategic communication centers in Pakistan would be targeted, thereby threatening its "capability of continuing as a socioeconomic entity." Chinese targets would be limited to six major industrial centers and two ports designed to service its SSBN fleet, thus threatening China's economic growth and its nuclear equation with the U.S. and Russia.[27] Metropolitan centers and ports would receive two strikes each of 1 megaton yield, battlefield targets two strikes of 15 kilotons each, dams one strike of 200–500 kilotons, and military airfields one strike of 20–50 kilotons. By carefully planning its nuclear doctrine and force structure in this manner, Nair suggests, India could capably deter a nuclear attack from Pakistan or China.

It hardly needs pointing out that seventeen nuclear strikes against Pakistan would have a catastrophic impact on the entire Indo-Gangetic Plain. We will analyze the environmental costs of going nuclear, and of the various capability levels within that policy option, later in the chapter. However, in the context of doctrine and capability, one must question the *credibility* of an Indian nuclear threat that if carried out would lethally poison the atmosphere, water sources, and topsoil of northern India with radioactive debris for centuries to come.

All Horizons

An all horizons nuclear capability, as the name suggests, is one that could strike anywhere on the planet. The nomenclature is derived from *tous azimuths*, the targeting doctrine of the French nuclear strike force, the *force de frappe*. No policymaker, opinion shaper, or analyst in India has ever publicly advocated an all horizons nuclear capability for India. Nevertheless, it is worth at least briefly considering for three reasons.

The first reason pertains to capabilities. To establish an all horizons capability India would have to develop an ICBM. Whether India has any intention of doing so, the PSLV (Polar Satellite Launch Vehicle) and GSLV (Geosynchronous Satellite Launch Vehicle) programs[28] of the Indian Space Research Organisation (ISRO) will give India that capability in a few years from now. The fact that this launch technology is being developed by ISRO, which functions within the Department of Space, rather than by the Integrated Missile Development Programme (IMDP) of the Defence Research and Development Organisation (DRDO) is unlikely to fool anyone. If India will soon have intercontinental means of delivery, it is important that the implications of this capability be examined.

The second reason for studying the all horizons capability is historical precedent. Apart from the U.S. and Russia, the other three nuclear weapons states have also built strategic nuclear forces consisting of ICBMs and SLBMs. The Chinese nuclear forces, the British "independent nuclear deterrent" (IND), and the French *force de frappe* all have *tous azimuths* capabilities. It would appear that any country that opts for a triad capability will soon find itself graduating to an all horizons capability.

The third reason for considering an all horizons capability has to do with the results of the Kroc Institute survey. Among the supporters of going nuclear, 35 percent favored developing a nuclear arsenal capable of striking *all* nuclear powers. Clearly there is substantial support among nuclear advocates for developing this maximum capability.

An all horizons posture would have to be grafted on to a triad system. An entirely new category of weapons systems, ICBMs and SLBMs, would be added to the country's strategic inventory. The C^3I required for an all horizons capability would need to be far more complicated and expensive than the system envisioned by Nair.

Costs and Feasibility

Assessing the costs and feasibility of going nuclear is an exercise fraught with complexity. For some proponents, the development of an overt Indian nuclear capability is worth any cost. Few support this maximalist approach, however. It is not a valid basis on which to make concrete policy choices. This analysis will examine the pluses and minuses of going nuclear per se, and the various capability levels within that broad option. The calculus will be based on five factors: *international, political, economic, environmental*, and *moral*.

International

If India were to opt to develop an overt nuclear capability, today or in the near future, the ramifications of this decision would be felt the world over. It would present the most significant challenge to the current NPT regime, and this would likely create a backlash that would not be in the interest of the country. It is theoretically possible that India could be incorporated within the treaty as a nuclear weapons state (NWS), but this is extremely unlikely. It is far more likely that serious pressure would be applied against India, not only by the nuclear weapons states but by all the major powers. As we have seen with Iraq, it is not difficult for the U.S., with the support of other great powers, to push the international community into isolating and severely punishing a recalcitrant state. Of course India is not an Iraq, and neither teaching a lesson to India nor making a lesson of India will be a particularly easy task. Furthermore, while nonaggression is a well-established international norm, nonproliferation is far less so. Nevertheless, unless at least one great power was willing to be in India's corner, the international configuration of forces would be inimical to India, and the consequences could be quite severe.

International sanctions against India at a time when the country is globalizing and liberalizing its economy could prove disastrous for India's economic, and perhaps even its political, stability. The sanctions would, predictably, target arms sales and oil supplies to India and Indian exports. Amitabh Mattoo has argued that sanctions against India to enforce nonproliferation policies would be unlikely and if attempted would likely be unsuccessful. For a big emerging market such as India, sanctions are a double-edged sword, and the U.S. might not be able to carry its allies along indefinitely.[29] But this assessment might not apply in an overt Indian decision to go nuclear. Such an act would be of very great concern internationally and would occasion a much stronger response than would the current policy of ambiguity. The severity of the international reaction would depend upon the capability level that India selects. An all horizons approach would seriously destabilize India's relations with the great powers. An emphasis on SSBNs would likely alienate India's neighbors in the Indian Ocean area. A minimal capability, on the other hand, would send a less aggressive message, but it would still raise Chinese concerns and would certainly provoke Pakistan to announce overt weaponization as well. A nonweaponized capability, on the other hand, would be far less threatening to the international community and might be a step the great powers could learn to accept.

Political

The domestic political impact of an Indian decision to go nuclear would depend upon the circumstances, external and internal, in which the decision is made. Let us consider external circumstances first. The Kroc Institute poll shows that many of those who support the current government policy of ambiguity would favor going nuclear if Pakistan were to test a bomb or if the nuclear weapons states threatened India. If Pakistan were to test a nuclear device, 48 percent of those supporting current policy felt that India would be justified in going nuclear. Faced with a threat from the nuclear weapons states, 52 percent of these respondents would favor India developing nuclear weapons. Other circumstances, such as a serious deterioration in relations with China or a threat of trade sanctions, did not pass muster with this group as justifications for going nuclear. The views of these supporters of official policy are especially important for assessing domestic political impact, since this was the largest group in the sample, constituting 57 percent of all respondents.

Apart from external circumstances, the domestic political impact of going nuclear would depend upon whether the decision was taken in consultation with the opposition parties or not. Inclusive and nonpartisan decision making would be far less divisive than a blatantly partisan approach on this critical issue. A decision to build the bomb solely to win political and electoral support would probably not work and could even be counterproductive. As the Kroc Institute poll shows, only one-third of the country's elite leaders favors going nuclear. There is far more support for maintaining a posture of ambiguity.

Much would depend upon which party took the decision to go nuclear. As the party of the political center, the Congress party would be better positioned to reap any political rewards and weather the criticisms that might arise from taking the nuclear step. The BJP, on the other hand, as a party of the Right, would probably face greater opposition for making such a decision. The Congress could respond by identifying the ambiguity option as the most appropriate and historically legitimate nuclear option for India, charging the BJP with recklessly exposing the country to external pressure. The communist parties could be counted on to criticize the actions and motives of a party whose ideology is completely antithetical to their own. What makes this assessment speculative is the rapidly changing nature of the Indian electoral landscape, marked by the emergence of caste-based politics, the consolidation of regional parties, and the steady "regionalization" of the older parties with nationwide support. How these new political developments might affect a decision to develop an overt nuclear capability is uncertain.

Relations between the civilian political and bureaucratic establishment on the one hand and the armed forces on the other are unlikely to be affected by any decision to go nuclear. Military subservience to civilian authority is a well-established characteristic of the Indian political system, and there is no reason to expect that the development of an overt nuclear capability would alter civil/military relations in the direction of greater military influence over policy formulation. On the contrary, going nuclear might shift the civil/military balance in favor of greater civilian involvement in military organization and doctrine. With a triad capability, the urgency of C^3I would imply far greater civilian participation in warfighting decisions, particularly decisions relating to conflict escalation.

An increase in state secrecy is another issue that is sometimes raised when the possibility of India's going nuclear is discussed. Secrecy is already all-pervasive in the Indian nuclear and security establishments. While a nuclear deterrent would certainly not increase government transparency, the system is already so opaque that any further deterioration seems unlikely.

Economic

Before examining the economic consequences of going nuclear, it is necessary to dispel a red herring that is frequently raised in these discussions, namely the "more bang for the buck" argument.[30] It is undeniable that nuclear weapons are less expensive than conventional weapons. There are few moving parts, and once the warhead is mated to the delivery vehicle, only routine checks of the casing and firing mechanisms are required. However, there are three lacunae in this analysis. The first is that nuclear weapons require highly skilled personnel, whose training and services therefore cost more than regular service personnel. The second is that the costs of extra security and radioactivity checks are considerable and must also be added to the nuclear weapons bill. However, it is the third lacuna that is by far the most significant, and that deserves more detailed examination.

Most of India's security threats require conventional forces, and in the case of internal security threats, paramilitary forces as well. In this crucial sense, nuclear weapons cannot *replace* conventional weapons; a hammer cannot be used to swat a fly. Earlier in this chapter, it was suggested in the "nuclear asymmetry" argument that only nuclear weapons could deter nuclear weapons. If that is true, the converse proposition is probably also valid: nuclear weapons deter *only* nuclear weapons, and conventional forces are needed to deal with conventional threats. Thus, irrespective of the nuclear capability level that India selects, its nuclear forces would be *additional* to its conventional forces. Some analysts argue that nuclear stability in the region could lead to a reduction in conventional forces. That may be the case, but no decision maker weighing the pros and cons of going nuclear can count on it happening. Moreover, if this process were to occur, it would be gradual and would probably take place slowly over many years.

What, then, would be the additional cost of an overt nuclear capability? Without engaging in extensive cost analysis, Subrahmanyam has suggested a figure of 100 billion rupees ($3 billion) at 1994 prices, which seems a reasonable estimate for the minimal capability level he favors. Nair engages in an extensive costing exercise and comes up with a figure of 68.35 billion rupees ($2.2 billion) at 1992 prices for the far more extravagant triad capability level he advocates. Clearly there is something missing in Nair's estimates. Indeed there are significant costs that Nair does not include in his calculations. He omits the huge costs of establishing nuclear plants and laboratory facilities and producing weapons-grade fissile material. Nair also excludes the cost of the SSBNs, the centerpiece of a triad capability, with the flimsy statement that "the cost factor for inducting nuclear powered submarines is already on the cards whether the country opts for a nuclear strategy or not."[31] This is an absurd argument, since SSBNs are perhaps the most expensive piece of military hardware in the world. The enormous research and development (R&D) costs and the vast production requirements of SSBNs must be included in the bill for a nuclear triad capability.

The cost of nuclear-capable aircraft, which are already part of the Indian inventory, is not factored into either Subrahmanyam's or Nair's calculations. What neither analyst considers, however, is the strong possibility that France, Britain, and Russia, the three suppliers of India's high-performance combat aircraft, would halt all further military supplies to India were it to go nuclear. The costs of attempting to design and build replacement aircraft would likely be staggering. The R&D and production costs of dual-use weaponry such as combat aircraft thus should be added to the bill for going nuclear.

The technical feasibility of the various capability levels still needs to be assessed. India's current ambiguity option coincides, in technological terms, to a nonweaponized capability. The only technology that India would need to incorporate into a nonweaponized regime would be the application of tags and sensors. For this, international technical assistance might be available since, as argued earlier, such a posture might enhance stability if applied bilaterally in a transparent manner. For minimal capability, India would need to fabricate nuclear warheads and perfect its ballistic missiles. Neither project should pose an insuperable technical problem for the Indian scientific establishment, although the financial costs would be considerable. A triad capability, on the other hand, would require the development and production of SSBNs, which would be a herculean task. The important point to note when analyzing economic and technical feasibility is that when the technology is neither extant nor readily obtainable from other sources, costs tend to rise toward infinity. This might well be the case for both the triad and all horizons options.

Environmental

The environmental costs involved in the production of nuclear weapons are similar to the environmental costs of civilian nuclear programs. However, there are several additional environmental costs involved in acquiring an overt nuclear weapons capability. They relate to nuclear tests, the possibility of accidents, the decommissioning of nuclear warheads, the cleanup of nuclear production facilities, and the impact of nuclear weapons if actually used. The degree of environmental impact would of course depend on the nuclear capability level.

The triad and all horizons options would be the most harmful to the environment. In both cases, regular nuclear testing, presumably underground, would be required. This would create hazards of radioactive contamination and generate considerable quantities of nuclear waste during normal operations. It would also create the additional risk of a venting of radioactive materials into the atmosphere during potential accidents. It is important to note that several accidents resulting in a substantial venting of radioactive fallout occurred during the U.S. and Soviet underground nuclear testing programs. Accidents have also occurred during U.S. and Soviet nuclear production activities, and the possibilities of such disasters in an Indian program cannot be dismissed. Even if major accidents can be avoided, the environmental challenge of decommissioning older weapons and cleaning up contaminated production facilities could be overwhelming. Again the experience of the United States and the Soviet Union in this regard is daunting. From an environmental perspective, the nonweaponized and minimal capabilities would be far more desirable. Although no nuclear capability can be, by definition, environmentally beneficial, the nonweaponized level is subject to the least risks in terms of nuclear accidents because the warheads are not deployed in battlefield conditions.

Until recently, the environmental cost of decommissioning nuclear weapons was a matter of national security for the nuclear weapons states and therefore not in the public domain. With the evaporation of the East/West nuclear standoff, this issue is now being openly debated. Estimates of the cost of environmental cleanup in U.S. nuclear weapons facilities alone range from $200 billion to $1 trillion.[32] The costs of addressing the far messier Soviet facilities have not even been estimated but are certain to be much higher. Any country that ventures into the business of producing nuclear weapons, India included, must anticipate staggering environmental challenges and costs.

The greatest impact of course would come from the actual use of nuclear weapons. Nuclear proponents argue that establishing an Indian nuclear deterrent will make the use of such weapons less likely, but the possibility that something might go wrong should not be discounted and must at least be considered. Much has been written in Japan and the West about the devastating consequences of nuclear war on human health and the environment.[33] There is no need to review this literature here. The horrifying, catastrophic effects of nuclear weapons are well known and widely accepted by scientists and policymakers alike. With South Asia these consequences would be even more immediate and inescapable, since the likely nuclear adversaries are contiguous geographic neighbors. As Rashid Naim has so graphically shown in an India/Pakistan nuclear exchange,[34] the country that launches a nuclear first strike would also suffer enormous destruction and environmental ruin, even in the unlikely event that the other side did not respond. Indian nuclear strikes against Pakistan would bring lethal clouds of radioactive fallout across northern India and cause widespread environmental contamination. If a nuclear attack by one side were reciprocated by the other, as appears likely, the entire subcontinent could become a radioactive wasteland.

Moral

How would India, a country professing global nuclear disarmament as a fundamental tenet of foreign policy, face the moral dilemmas that confront a nuclear weapons state? Some may argue that such moral issues have no relevance to strategic policy, that these are matters for religious leaders and not statespersons. Yet moral legitimacy and credibility are important ingredients of political authority and cannot be dismissed easily. For Nehru, the espousal of nuclear disarmament had very practical purposes apart from its moral appeal. Through this policy India sought, and partially achieved, leadership among the developing nations of the world. India claimed to speak for the earth's nonnuclear majority in demanding that the nuclear powers give up these weapons of mass destruction. Admittedly, India's purity in this regard was considerably tarnished following the 1974 nuclear test at Pokhran, but even afterwards and continuing to this day New Delhi has maintained a strong voice of condemnation against the nuclear arms race. To reverse course and abandon this long-held tenet of Indian foreign policy would not be cost-free. India would lose face internationally and at home might face opposition from those people of conscience who still believe in the moral legitimacy of the non-nuclear option.

Conclusion

Of the four levels of nuclear capability that have been analyzed in this chapter, some are clearly more politically plausible, militarily credible, and cost-effective than others. The easiest option to dismiss on economic and political grounds is the all horizons capability level. This policy choice would send India on a collision course not just with the other nuclear powers but also with the economic powerhouses of the world. Not only would the United States, Russia, Britain, France, and China respond negatively, but Japan and Germany would undoubtedly back sanctions and other punitive measures as well. These countries would not sit back and watch idly if India were to embark on a worldwide nuclear weapons capability.

The triad capability option also has severe problems associated with it. The development of the sea leg of the triad would be technically difficult and financially impoverishing. Even if India were able, at great cost, to develop SSBNs, this would lead to the alienation of the countries with which India shares the Indian Ocean littoral. Neither a no first use pledge nor a targeting doctrine aimed solely at Pakistan and China would be likely to calm the apprehensions of Indonesia, Australia, and South Africa, countries with a technological potential to match India's. A nuclear arms race in the Indian Ocean might well be the consequence of such a decision by India.

A minimal nuclear capability would avoid many of the costs of the more grandiose options. A Pokhran-type warhead would not need further testing. The minimal option would not involve the development of expensive new delivery systems. It would not pose a threat to countries beyond the region. The financial costs would be less prohibitive.

The problem with the minimal capability is that it makes too many uncertain assumptions about Pakistan's reactions. Just because India chooses not to develop a doctrine of warfare, this does not guarantee that Pakistan will follow suit. On the contrary, Pakistan would have very good reasons to integrate its nuclear arsenal into its military structure and develop a convincing nuclear warfare doctrine. The North Atlantic Treaty Organization (NATO), faced with an overwhelming Warsaw Pact conventional superiority in the Central European theater, developed an intricate doctrinal architecture to convince the other side that it *would use* nuclear weapons if push came to shove. There is no reason to believe that Pakistan, in the face of a similar Indian conventional superiority, would not act in a similar fashion. This in turn would spark an upwardly spiraling nuclear arms race akin to the U.S./Soviet competition that would lead to higher levels of weaponry.

The nonweaponized capability would therefore appear to have the field almost to itself. It is free from the flaws inherent in the other options. The basic problem with the nonweaponized option is that it requires levels of trust, openness, and cooperation that are sorely lacking from the current reality of India/Pakistan relations. The technology certainly exists for a nonweaponized capability. Whether the political will exists to make it work is quite another matter. In recent years, Indian and Pakistani political parties have exhibited more factionalism than maturity, due in the former case to the steady unraveling of consensual politics and in the latter case to the lack of democratic consolidation. These trends bode ill for the installation of a nonweaponized nuclear regime in both countries.

The exclusion of China from the equation is another major problem and reason a nonweaponized capability may not be acceptable to India.

Ultimately, external factors may be the major determinants of India's decision whether to go nuclear. In particular, India's policy options will be determined by the progress (or lack thereof) toward comprehensive nuclear disarmament at the global level. As the Kroc Institute poll confirms, the single greatest factor that could persuade both nuclear proponents and supporters of current policy to forgo the nuclear option would be a time-bound plan for global nuclear disarmament. A commitment by the nuclear powers to fulfill their obligations under the Nuclear Nonproliferation Treaty to negotiate in good faith for nuclear disarmament would greatly reduce the likelihood of a nuclear weapons future for South Asia. As long as the nuclear powers continue to hold on to these weapons the temptation will remain for India to go nuclear.

Notes

1. Literally, the "line of Lakshmana." In the *Ramayana*, one of the two great epics that form an important cornerstone of Indian (and particularly Hindu) culture, Lakshmana drew a line around Sita within which no evil force could harm her in his absence. Although he bade her to stay within the line, she stepped over it and was promptly abducted by the demon-king Ravana.

2. See Waldo Stumpf, "South Africa's Nuclear Weapons Programme," (paper prepared for the conference on "Proliferation: A Cost/Benefit Analysis," New Delhi, 8–9 November 1993).

3. When Enrico Fermi's team achieved the first controlled nuclear chain reaction on 2 December 1942, Arthur H. Compton passed on the news to James B. Conant with the words "the Italian navigator has just landed in the new world." When Indira Gandhi received the message "The Buddha Smiles" in May 1974, she knew that India's nuclear test at Pokhran had been successful.

4. See K. Subrahmanyam, "Implications of Nuclear Asymmetry," in *Nuclear Myths and Realities: India's Dilemma*, ed. K. Subrahmanyam (New Delhi: ABC Publishing, 1981). The problem of nuclear asymmetry has also been studied within the Indian armed forces. See "Effects of Nuclear Asymmetry on Conventional Deterrence," Combat Paper No. 1, College of Combat, Mhow, India, May 1981.

5. Quoted in Ziba Moshaver, *Nuclear Weapons Proliferation in the Indian Subcontinent* (New York: St. Martin's Press, 1991), 63.

6. *The Dawn*, Karachi, 24 August 1994.

7. *The Dawn*, Karachi, 28 August, 1994.

8. President Bhutto wrote in his prison memoirs: "The Christian, Jewish, Hindu civilizations have this capability. The Communist powers also possess it. Only the Islamic civilization was without it, but that position was about to change." Zulfikar A. Bhutto, *If I Am Assassinated* (New Delhi: Vikas Publishing House, 1979), 138.

9. K. Sundarji, *Blind Men of Hindoostan: Indo-Pak Nuclear War* (New Delhi: UBS Publishers, 1993), 215–16.

10. IDR Research Team, "Nuclear China: The Equation with India," *Indian Defence Review*, July 1989, 94.

11. K. Subrahmanyam, "Nuclear Force Design and Minimum Deterrence Strategy for India," in *Future Imperilled: India's Security in the 1990s and Beyond*, ed. Bharat Karnad (New Delhi: Viking, 1994), 186. For a flavor of Indian thinking on this matter during the cold war period, see Air Chief Marshal P.C. Lal's brief reference to the Chinese nuclear threat and countervailing superpower pressure in his National Security Lecture of 21–22 March 1975 in P.C. Lal, *Some Problems of Defence* (New Delhi: United Service Institution of India, 1977), 94.

12. Vijai K. Nair, *Nuclear India* (New Delhi: Lancers, 1992), 16–17.

13. K. Subrahmanyam, "Nuclear Force Design," 178.

14. Literally, "Weapon of Brahma." In the Hindu Trinity, Brahma is the Creator, Vishnu the Protector, and Shiva the Destroyer.

15. See J.N. Chaudhury, *India's Problems of National Security in the Seventies* (New Delhi: United Service Institution of India, 1973), 17–24.

16. See, for instance, an article by the IDR Research Team, "Grappling with the Dynamics on Nuclear Strategy: Policy Formulation for a Nuclear India," *Indian Defence Review*, July 1989, 49–56.

17. Cited in Ashok Kapur, *India's Nuclear Option: Atomic Diplomacy and Decision Making* (New York: Praeger, 1976), 193–94.

18. Raja Ramanna, "Limits and Limitations," in Raja Ramanna, *National Security and Modern Technology* (New Delhi: United Service Institution of India, 1988), 61.

19. Apart from these four nuclear capability levels, the notion of a *recessed* deterrence (also known as "virtual weaponization") has been expounded by Air Commodore Jasjit Singh. See Jasjit Singh, "Prospects for Nuclear Proliferation," in *Nuclear Deterrence: Problems and Perspectives in the 1990's*, ed. Serge Sur (New York: United Nations, 1993), 66. Singh suggests that there are a number of states, among them India, which do not have a nuclear weapons program but which nevertheless have a nuclear technology base which is more than adequate to achieve weaponization at short notice. However, it is open to debate whether a recessed nuclear capability, which implies nothing more than the possession of requisite technology, amounts to "going nuclear." To go back to our definition at the beginning of this chapter, going nuclear involves development, deployment, and declaration of nuclear weapons capability. In other words, it is not sufficient for the *level of technology* alone to be overt. In policy terms, a recessed or virtual nuclear capability that is overt is likely to closely resemble, and perhaps be indistinguishable from, a nonweaponized nuclear capability. It is for this reason that a recessed capability is not treated in our analysis as a distinct level of going nuclear.

20. See George Perkovich, "A Nuclear Third Way in South Asia," *Foreign Policy* no. 91 (Summer 1993): 85–104. A later (and longer) version of this article is George Perkovich, "Three Models for Nuclear Policy in South Asia: The Case for Non-Weaponised Deterrence," in *The Road Ahead: Indo-US Strategic Dialogue*, ed. Jasjit Singh (New Delhi: Lancers International, 1994), 89–123.

21. K. Sundarji, "Indian Nuclear Doctrine-II: Sino-Indo-Pak Triangle," *Indian Express*, 26 November 1994, 8.

22. K. Subrahmanyam, "Nuclear Force Design," 176–95.

23. Payload of 500–1,000 kg and a range of 150–250 km.

24. Payload of 1 ton and a range of 2,500 km.
25. K. Subrahmanyam, "Nuclear Force Design," 189.
26. Nair, *Nuclear India*.
27. Ibid., 144–45.
28. If adapted in a ballistic missile role, the PSLV could carry a 1 ton payload over a distance of 8,000 km, while a GSLV could carry a 2.5 ton payload over a distance of 14,000 km.
29. See Amitabh Mattoo, "Sanctions, Incentives and Nuclear Proliferation: The Case of India," *Journal of Peace Studies* 1, no. 3 (July/August 1994).
30. See Kanti Bajpai and Varun Sahni, "Secure and Solvent: Thinking About an Affordable Defence for India," RGICS Paper No. 11 (New Delhi: Rajiv Gandhi Institute for Contemporary Studies, May 1994): 25–28.
31. Nair, *Nuclear India*, 205.
32. Robert Barker, "Costs of US Nuclear Weapons Program," (paper prepared for the conference on "Proliferation: A Cost/Benefit Analysis," New Delhi: 8–9 November 1993).
33. See *Study on the Climatic and Other Global Effects of Nuclear War*, A/43/351, Department for Disarmament Affairs, Report to the Secretary General, New York: United Nations, 1989; Committee for the Compilation of Materials on Damage Caused by the Atomic Bombs in Hiroshima and Nagasaki, *Hiroshima and Nagasaki: The Physical, Medical, and Social Effects of the Atomic Bombings*, trans. Eisei Ishikawa and David L. Swain (New York: Basic Books, 1981).
34. Rashid Naim, "After Midnight," in *Nuclear Proliferation in South Asia*, ed. Stephen P. Cohen (Boulder, Colo.: Westview, 1991), 23–61.

Appendices

Appendix A

An Analysis of the Kroc Institute Survey

Jackie G. Smith

As noted in chapter 1, this study was designed to identify the views of India's nuclear weapons policy held by Indian elites. The survey consisted of interviews with educated elites in seven Indian cities. Respondents were government bureaucrats, academicians, scientists, journalists, lawyers, politicians, doctors, members of the police and armed forces, and arts and sports figures. Interviews were administered by MARG Marketing and Research Group (New Delhi) for the Joan B. Kroc Institute for International Peace Studies. The target sample size was one thousand; 992 of those approached responded. The sample was selected randomly from publicly available lists of professionals and public figures, including professional association lists and public telephone directories. The sample was stratified to reflect proportions of elite categories in the general population. Academics and political elites were slightly oversampled, as their views are presumably of greater political significance. The arts/sports and social category—far less relevant to public awareness and debate on international policy—was undersampled. Respondents were interviewed in Delhi, Bombay, Calcutta, Madras, Bangalore, Lucknow, and Hyderabad between late September and early November 1994.

Demographics

Chapter 1 pointed out that respondents' answers varied little from city to city. Biographic characteristics also bore little relationship to the respondents' opinions on nuclear policy, although the few women elites among the pool of respondents were less likely than the vast majority of male respondents to favor nuclear weapons development. Occupation did not appear to have a substantive effect on one's views on nuclear weapons policy. Also, those respondents claiming to have marginal or significant influence on India's nuclear policy were slightly more likely to support India's current policy or to support India's acquisition of nuclear weapons.[1] This may be because several respondents in this category were employed by the government.

Views on India's Nuclear Policy

Below are the raw distributions of responses to questions about respondents' views on India's nuclear policy. Respondents were divided into three groups; the first and largest group consisted of those supporting India's current policy (N=563), the second group supported India's acquisition of nuclear weapons (N=326), and the third group favored India's renunciation of nuclear weapons (N=83). Figure 1 illustrates these proportions:

FIGURE 1: View on India's Nuclear Policy
Kroc Institute Survey, 11/94

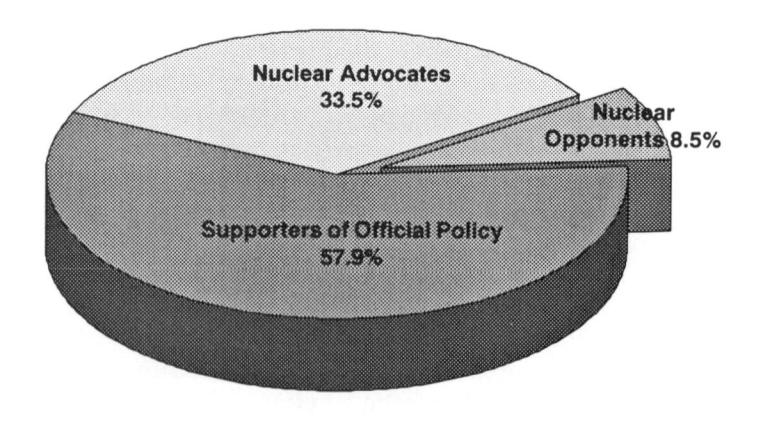

- Nuclear Advocates 33.5%
- Nuclear Opponents 8.5%
- Supporters of Official Policy 57.9%

Support for Multilateral Arms Control

A substantial portion of elite respondents indicated support for India's participation in international treaties regulating the spread and possession of nuclear weapons. Thirty-nine percent indicated support for India's participation in the Nuclear Nonproliferation Treaty (NPT), despite India's long and principled opposition to that regime. Of this 39 percent, 13 percent called for such a move even without parallel steps by Pakistan. More than twice as many respondents supported an international treaty for the elimination of nuclear weapons.

Appendix A: An Analysis of the Kroc Institute Survey 111

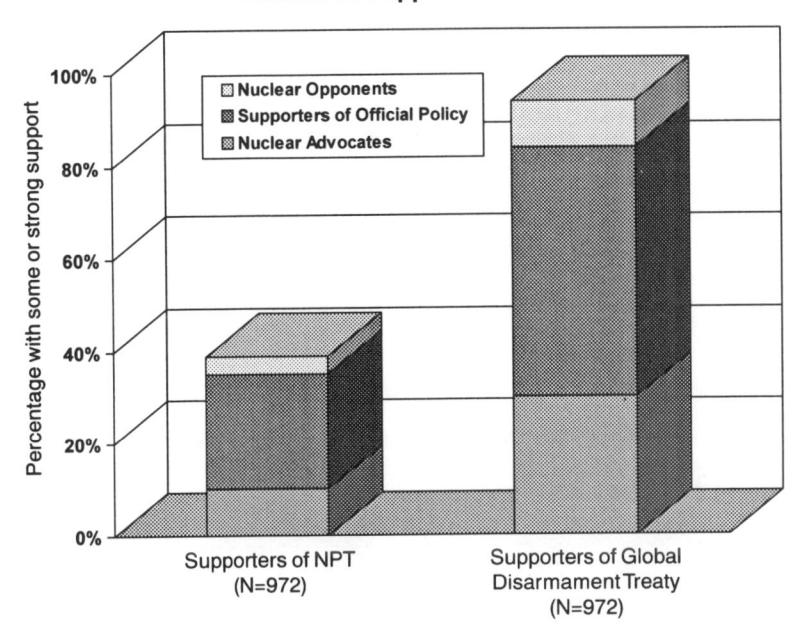

FIGURE 2: Support for Nuclear Treaties

[Bar chart showing percentage with some or strong support for Supporters of NPT (N=972) and Supporters of Global Disarmament Treaty (N=972), broken down by Nuclear Opponents, Supporters of Official Policy, and Nuclear Advocates]

As seen in figure 2, 39 percent of all respondents favored India's signing of the Nuclear Nonproliferation Treaty, either with or without the condition that Pakistan also joins the regime. Support for the NPT was strongest among nuclear opponents, with 54 percent favoring this treaty. In addition, 42 percent of those supporting India's official policy (which is opposed to the NPT) showed support for India's participation in the treaty. One-third of the pronuclear group also backed the NPT.

Overall, 94 percent of respondents supported the signing of an international treaty banning nuclear weapons. This support was fairly consistent among all three policy preference groups: Among the group supporting India's current nuclear weapons policy, 96 percent supported an international agreement for the elimination of all nuclear weapons. Those respondents who supported India's acquisition of nuclear weapons were not dramatically less supportive of multilateral arms control efforts, and 91 percent supported a multilateral nuclear disarmament treaty. Together, these data show considerable public support for India's participation in multilateral nuclear arms control efforts.

The United States Information Agency (USIA) surveys of Indian college graduates taken between 1989 and 1995 further suggested that domestic support for India's participation in the NPT regime varies inversely with respondents' perceptions of relations with Pakistan. In other words, when fewer respondents viewed bilateral relations as fairly or very poor, more support for the NPT was observed. When relations were perceived less favorably in the early 1990s, support for the treaty declined further. Figure 3 illustrates this pattern:

FIGURE 3: Support for NPT and View of Indo-Pakistani Relations

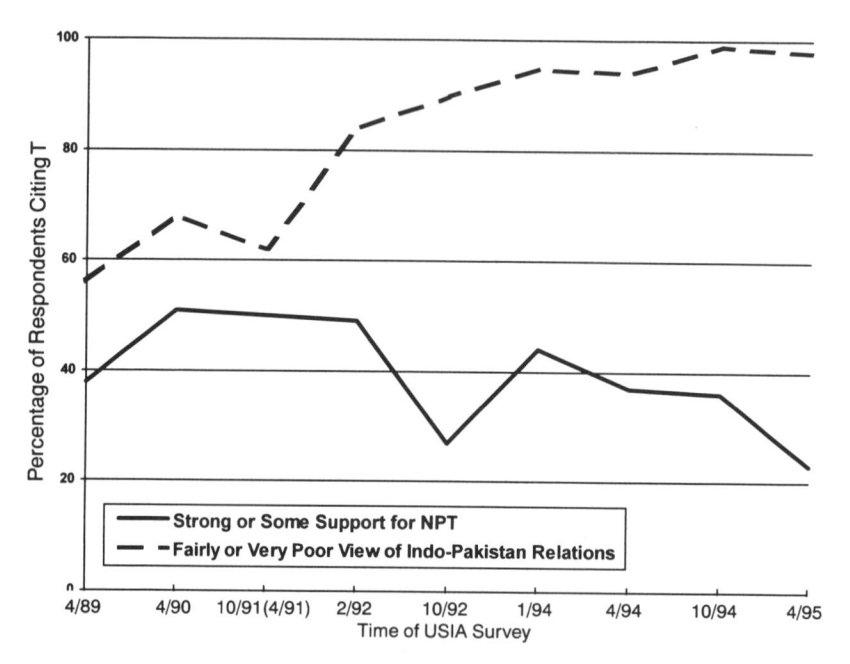

[Graph showing Percentage of Respondents Citing T on y-axis (0-100) vs. Time of USIA Survey on x-axis (4/89, 4/90, 10/91 (4/91), 2/92, 10/92, 1/94, 4/94, 10/94, 4/95), with two lines: "Strong or Some Support for NPT" and "Fairly or Very Poor View of Indo-Pakistan Relations"]

While the Kroc Institute data show that there is strong support among Indian elites for both the NPT and especially for a global nuclear treaty, the USIA data suggest that such support might be even stronger if perceptions of Indo-Pakistani relations were improved through, for instance, regional confidence-building measures or a bilateral nuclear test ban agreement.

Figure 4 illustrates the pattern of responses to the questions, Could anything justify India's developing nuclear weapons? (asked of supporters of official policy and nuclear opponents) and Why should India develop nuclear weapons? (asked of nuclear advocates). Threats from a nuclear Pakistan were most frequently seen to justify such an escalation of India's defensive posture. More than 40 percent of all respondents (and the largest proportion of official policy supporters and of nuclear opponents) saw threats from other nuclear powers[2] as requiring a nuclear de-

Appendix A: An Analysis of the Kroc Institute Survey 113

terrent, and less than 20 percent of respondents saw China as posing such a threat.

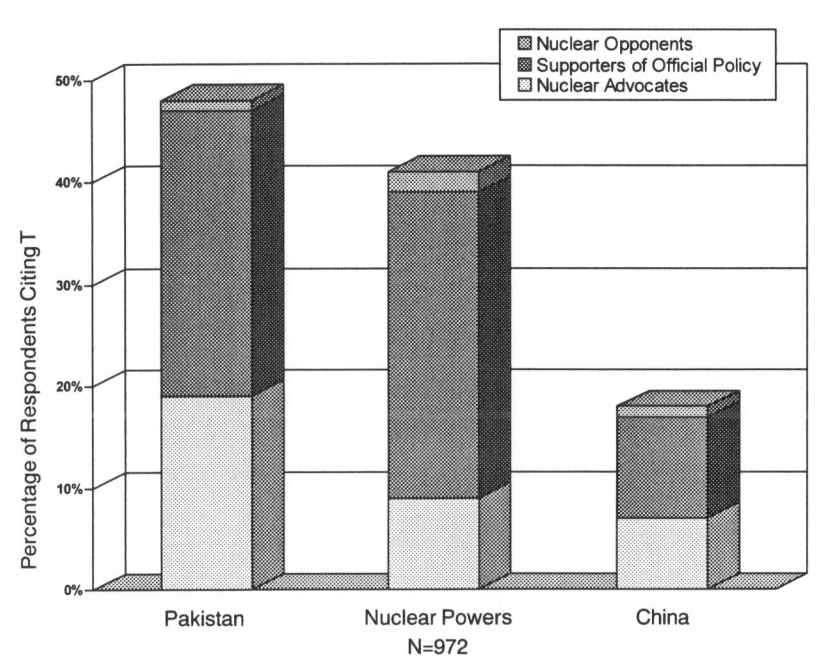

FIGURE 4: Perceptions of Threats Requiring Nuclear Deterrent

The data in figure 4 are instructive for understanding the perceptions among India's elites of India's major nuclear security threats. Nearly as many elites saw threats from nuclear powers as a justification for nuclear weapons development as threats from a nuclear Pakistan. This finding suggests that Western nuclear policies may be nearly as responsible for insecurity as are regional tensions.

Respondents were also asked to indicate which circumstances they thought would justify India's actual use of nuclear weapons. Table 1 presents the responses to this question. Overall, 44 percent of the respondents felt that nuclear weapons should never be used. Thirty-three percent of all respondents felt that the use of nuclear weapons would be justified if Pakistan attempted to take over Kashmir. The next largest segment (27 percent) felt that nuclear weapons use was justified if a U.S.-led coalition of countries intervened militarily in India's affairs. Twenty-three percent felt that a nuclear response was appropriate if China invaded the country.

TABLE 1: Perceived Threats Justifying Nuclear Weapons*

Q15: Threats justifying nuclear weapons use	Supporters of Official Policy (N=563)	Nuclear Advocates (N=326)	Nuclear Opponents (N=83)
(Figures below are percentages)			
Pakistan	30	45	11
U.S. Intervention	25	30	21
China	24	26	6
No Circumstance	46	33	74

*Column totals exceed 100% due to multiple responses on this question.

As may be expected, those respondents who believed that India should incorporate nuclear weapons into its arsenal were more likely to view threats from Pakistan, China and an international intervention as justifying a nuclear response. Yet, 33 percent of those supporting India's adoption of nuclear weapons saw no circumstance as justifying their use. Of those opposed to nuclear weapons, 38 percent indicated situations that would justify their use, most citing a U.S.-led international military intervention. The overall pattern of perceptions of threats requiring a nuclear response reflects the general pattern of views on threats justifying the development of nuclear weapons presented above: While Pakistan is most frequently cited as the primary concern, threats from nuclear powers—particularly the U.S.—are secondary and China ranks lowest among these three threats. However, while most respondents cited specific situations that would justify India's development of nuclear weapons, nearly half (44 percent) of all respondents saw no circumstance that would justify their use.

Factors Shaping Views

A major concern of this study is to determine what factors would motivate respondents favoring some form of nuclear option (either nuclear ambiguity or outright nuclear weapons development) to change their positions on India's nuclear policy. Those supporting India's current position were asked about what would motivate them to support India's

Appendix A: An Analysis of the Kroc Institute Survey 115

renunciation of nuclear weapons. Those favoring the acquisition of nuclear weapons were asked what might lead them to back away from this position.

It has been noted in several chapters of this volume and restated in figure 4 and table 1 above that threats from a nuclear Pakistan, from other nuclear powers, and from a deterioration in relations with China were perceived by most respondents as justifying a shift to nuclear weapons development. These same threats were also cited as possibly justifying India's use of nuclear weapons. As is shown in figure 5, these same considerations were related to responses on the question of what could lead India away from the further development of its nuclear defense.

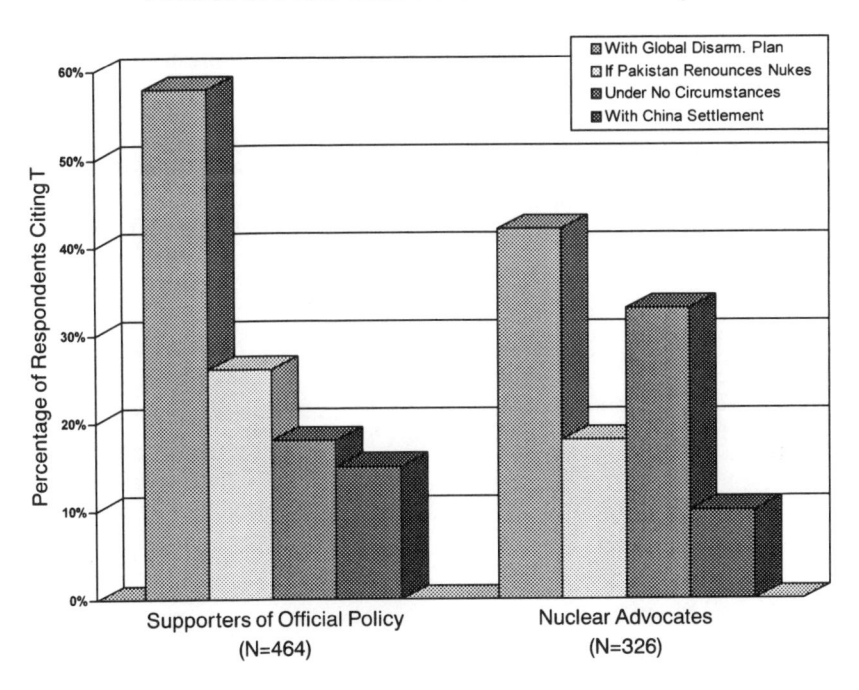

FIGURE 5: Could India Renounce Nuclear Weapons?

[Bar chart showing Percentage of Respondents Citing T for Supporters of Official Policy (N=464) and Nuclear Advocates (N=326), with categories: With Global Disarm. Plan, If Pakistan Renounces Nukes, Under No Circumstances, With China Settlement]

Figure five shows that both nuclear advocates and those supporting official policy felt that a global plan for nuclear disarmament would justify India's renunciation of nuclear weapons. Interestingly, more pro-nuclear respondents felt that a global disarmament plan could justify the abandonment of nuclear ambitions (42 percent) than saw no circumstances as justifying a nuclear abstinence policy (33 percent). Considerable proportions of both groups (26 percent of official supporters and 18 percent of nuclear advocates) saw a verifiable renunciation of Pakistan's nuclear option as a condition meriting a similar move by India. A somewhat smaller proportion of both groups cited an agreement with China in response to this question.

In sum, this survey of a range of Indian elites indicates that there is a reasonable amount of support for more conciliatory nuclear policies. In particular, large proportions of those favoring some form of nuclear deterrent, either explicitly or through strategic ambiguity, were likely to abandon this support if a global nuclear disarmament plan could be achieved. Similarly, a reduction of Indo-Pakistani and, to a smaller extent, Indo-Chinese tensions would increase elite support for India's renunciation of its nuclear option.

Notes

1. The correlation coefficients between influence on nuclear policy and opinion—while statistically significant—are quite small ($r= .154$ and $r= .103$, respectively).

2. The wording of the survey question can imply the inclusion of China as a nuclear power, although the fact that less than twenty percent of respondents explicitly cited a breakdown in relations with China in response to this question suggests that their implication is that the threat here is from Western nuclear powers.

Appendix B

Complete Results and Tabular Data of the Kroc Institute Opinion Survey

TABLE 1: Stance on Nuclear Issues
Questions 6 and 23

	All	Arts/ Sports/ Social	Acad./ Science	Bur./ Diplo- matic	Busi.	Jour.	Law	Med.	Armed Forces/ Police
Base (in actual numbers):	992	43	165	145	112	167	74	57	154
(Figures below are percentages)									
Supporters of Official Policy India should maintain its official position on nuclear issues	57	42	54	61	51	58	55	56	64
Nuclear Advocates India should develop nuclear weapons	33	32	36	25	41	29	39	35	30
Nuclear Opponents India should renounce nuclear weapons	8	21	10	7	7	12	5	7	3
No Opinion	2	5	–	7	1	1	1	2	3

TABLE 2: Rating of Issues
Questions 1, 2, and 6

	All	Supporters of Official Policy	Nuclear Advocates	Nuclear Opponents
Base (in actual numbers):	992	563	326	83
(Figures below are percentages)				
Communalism	52	54	47	60
Poverty	47	50	40	57
Economic stability	36	37	36	29
Terrorism	30	30	34	23
Kashmir	15	13	18	12
GATT	8	8	9	10
Nuclear issue	6	4	8	4
U.S. support to Pakistan	4	3	6	5
Forex reserves	3	2	3	2
Percent considering nuclear issue very important	41	37	49	40

Appendix B: Complete Results and Tabular Data of the Kroc Institute Survey

TABLE 3: Availability of Information on Nuclear Issues
Question 4

	All	Supporters of Official Policy	Nuclear Advocates	Nuclear Opponents
Base (in actual numbers):	992	563	326	83
(Figures below are percentages)				
Information on nuclear issues is easily available	13	13	12	10
Information on nuclear issues is not easy to get	40	39	41	41
Information on nuclear issues is neither easy nor difficult to get	20	21	20	19
Information on nuclear issues is difficult to get	21	20	24	23
Information on nuclear issues is almost impossible to get	6	7	4	7

TABLE 4: Level of Knowledge About Nuclear Policy
Question 3

	All	Supporters of Official Policy	Nuclear Advocates	Nuclear Opponents
Base (in actual numbers):	992	563	326	83
(Figures below are percentages)				
India's nuclear policy is a major area of interest for me professionally	10	8	14	8
I am well informed about India's nuclear policy	28	30	24	25
I am informed about India's nuclear policy just enough	44	44	44	41
I am not really informed about India's nuclear policy	11	11	11	15
I have never really paid any attention to India's nuclear policy	7	7	7	11

Appendix B: Complete Results and Tabular Data of the Kroc Institute Survey 121

TABLE 5: Influence on Nuclear Policy
Question 18

	All	Supporters of Official Policy	Nuclear Advocates	Nuclear Opponents
Base (in actual numbers):	**992**	**563**	**326**	**83**
(Figures below are percentages)				
I have significant influence on India's nuclear policy	5	5	5	4
I have marginal influence on India's nuclear policy	12	12	12	18
I have no influence on India's nuclear policy	33	35	30	32
I am not related in any way to India's nuclear policy	50	29	53	46

**TABLE 6: Opinion About Civilian Nuclear Energy Program
("Strongly Agree" and "Somewhat Agree")
Question 5**

	All	Supporters of Official Policy	Nuclear Advocates	Nuclear Opponents
Base (in actual numbers):	992	563	326	83
(Figures below are percentages)				
Civilian nuclear energy program can help meet India's energy deficit	87	88	87	85
The benefits of a civilian nuclear energy program far outweigh its cost	60	63	58	52
A civilian nuclear energy program can be more harmful than beneficial	26	24	27	40
The costs of a civilian nuclear energy program far outweigh its benefits	21	21	21	28
A civilian nuclear energy program has high environmental costs attached	60	61	61	64

Appendix B: Complete Results and Tabular Data of the Kroc Institute Survey

TABLE 7: Could India Renounce Nuclear Weapons Under Any Circumstance?
Questions 8a and 11a

	Supporters of Official Policy	Nuclear Advocates
Base (in actual numbers):	464	326
(Figures below are percentages)		
A final boundary settlement with China and the removal of Chinese nuclear weapons from Tibet	15	10
A verifiable renunciation of Pakistan's nuclear option	26	18
Nuclear protection from the U.S. and/or Russia	6	4
Threat of international sanctions	7	8
A time-bound plan for global nuclear disarmament	58	42
A permanent seat on the UN Security Council	12	14
Guaranteed access to advanced technology	9	7
Diplomatic & political support for India's position on Kashmir	8	7
Under no circumstances	18	33

**TABLE 8: Should India Sign the Nuclear Nonproliferation Treaty?
Questions 8b and 11b**

	Supporters of Official Policy	Nuclear Advocates
Base (in actual numbers):	**464**	**219**
(Figures below are percentages)		
Unilaterally	17	16
Only if Pakistan also does the same	35	31
Under no circumstances	49	52
Cannot say	–	1

Appendix B: Complete Results and Tabular Data of the Kroc Institute Survey

TABLE 9: Why India Should Develop Nuclear Weapons
Question 9

	Nuclear Advocates
Base (in actual numbers):	**326**
(Figures below are percentages)	
Threats from nuclear Pakistan	57
To improve India's bargaining power in world affairs	49
To enhance India's international status	38
Threats from other nuclear powers	27
Threats from China	20
Increased international pressures on India's domestic policies	18
Threats of trade sanctions	6

TABLE 10: Should India Sign the Nuclear Nonproliferation Treaty?
Question 12

	Nuclear Opponents
Base (in actual numbers):	**83**
(Figures below are percentages)	
Unilaterally and sign the NPT	24
Unilaterally and not sign the NPT	17
Bilaterally with Pakistan & sign the NPT together	30
Bilaterally with Pakistan & not sign the NPT	4
Jointly with Pakistan and China	25

Appendix B: Complete Results and Tabular Data of the Kroc Institute Survey

TABLE 11: Why India Should Renounce Nuclear Weapons
Question 13

	Nuclear Opponents
Base (in actual numbers):	83
(Figures below are percentages)	
Nuclear weapons are morally repugnant	46
A nuclear India would become the target of the major nuclear powers	18
Nuclear weapons do not address the primary threats to India's security, i.e., terrorism and insurgency	29
India cannot afford nuclear weapons	34
Nuclear weapons production harms the environment	41

TABLE 12: Could Anything Justify India's Developing Nuclear Weapons? Questions 7 and 14

	Supporters of Official Policy	Nuclear Opponents
Base (in actual numbers):	563	83
(Figures below are percentages)		
Threats from other nuclear powers	52	22
Pakistan tests a nuclear device	48	10
Increased international pressures on India's domestic policies	18	2
A serious deterioration in relations with China	17	6
Kashmir on the verge of secession	12	2
A breakdown of India's relations with Western countries	10	7
Increased turmoil in the country requiring a new rallying symbol for national unity	8	2
Threats of trade sanctions	6	2
Under no circumstances	13	60

TABLE 13: Extent of Developing Nuclear Weapons
Question 10

	Nuclear Advocates
Base (in actual numbers):	**326**

(Figures below in percentages)

Develop a nuclear arsenal capable of striking China and Pakistan	19
Develop a nuclear arsenal capable of striking only Pakistan	12
Develop a nuclear arsenal capable of striking all nuclear powers	35
Develop all components but not actually assemble any nuclear weapon	34

TABLE 14: When Could India Use Nuclear Weapons?
Question 15

	All	Supporters of Official Policy	Nuclear Advocates	Nuclear Opponents
Base (in actual numbers):	972	563	326	83
(Figures below are percentages)				
If Pakistan were about to take over Kashmir	33	30	45	11
If China were about to overwhelm India militarily	23	24	26	6
If a U.S.–led coalition of countries were to intervene militarily	27	25	30	21
Accidentally	4	4	5	2
Never	44	46	33	74

Appendix B: Complete Results and Tabular Data of the Kroc Institute Survey 131

TABLE 15: Extent of Support for International Agreement Eliminating Nuclear Weapons
Question 16

	All	Supporters of Official Policy	Nuclear Advocates	Nuclear Opponents
Base (in actual numbers):	972	563	326	83
(Figures below are percentages)				
Totally support	83	88	76	86
Support to an extent	11	9	15	8
Neither support nor oppose	3	2	5	2
Oppose to an extent	1	1	2	–
Totally oppose	2	1	2	4

TABLE 16: When Will an International Treaty Be Signed?
Question 17

	All	Supporters of Official Policy	Nuclear Advocates	Nuclear Opponents
Base (in actual numbers):	**972**	**563**	**326**	**83**
(Figures below in percentages)				
The next five years	22	22	18	37
The next ten years	25	26	23	27
The next twenty years	15	17	12	16
Never	36	33	45	18
Don't know	2	2	3	2

TABLE 17: Demographic Profile
Questions 20, 21, 22a, and 25

	All	Supporters of Official Policy	Nuclear Advocates	Nuclear Opponents
Base (in actual numbers):	992	563	326	83

(Figures below in percentages)

	All	Supporters of Official Policy	Nuclear Advocates	Nuclear Opponents
Sex:				
Male	91	92	91	84
Female	9	8	9	16
Age:				
Up to 39 years	20	19	21	25
40 to 49 years	32	31	34	28
50 to 59 years	35	36	35	31
60 years or over	13	14	10	16
Education:				
Graduate (Gen.)	18	16	19	18
Graduate (Prof.)	11	11	13	10
Post Graduate (Gen.)	27	27	29	19
Post Graduate (Prof.)	27	29	26	25
Doctorate	15	16	12	22
Others	–	–	1	2
Awards Received:				
Academy Awards (e.g., Sahitya Academy)	4	4	3	5
National awards	5	6	4	8
Academic field	1	–	2	1
Other (claimed)	17	18	17	12
None	73	71	75	74

TABLE 18: Political Affiliation
Question 19

	All	Supporters of Official Policy	Nuclear Advocates	Nuclear Opponents
Base (in actual numbers):	992	563	326	83
(Figures below are percentages)				
Cong. (I)	25	26	25	21
BJP	13	11	18	5
JD	1	1	–	4
CPI/CPM	4	4	2	7
SJP/BSP	1	1	1	–
T. Desam	–	–	–	2
AIADMK	1	1	1	–
DMK	–	–	1	–
Shiv Sena/RSS	–	1	1	–
None	51	51	49	53
Refused	3	3	3	5

Appendix C
MARG Survey Questions

Q.1 (See Table 2)

There are various issues which are being discussed and considered important by different people. I have some of them listed here. Please take a look at this card and tell me which of these issues/problems facing our country today do you consider to be most important, next important, etc.? (Continued until respondent ranked five.)

ISSUE/PROBLEM
Communalism
Economic stability
Kashmir
Forex reserves
Nuclear issue
GATT
U.S. support to Pakistan
Terrorism
Poverty

Q.2 (See Table 2)

Focusing on the nuclear issue, how important do you personally find it to be? Please respond with the help of this card.

Very important
Somewhat important
Neither important nor unimportant
Somewhat unimportant
Very unimportant

Q.3 (See Table 4)

Which of these statements is most true about you?

> India's nuclear policy is a major area of interest for me professionally
> I am well informed about India's nuclear policy
> I am informed about India's nuclear policy but just enough
> I am not really informed about India's nuclear policy
> I have never really paid any attention to India's nuclear policy

Q.4 (See Table 3)

Often we might really find it difficult to get information on certain issues while information on others is very readily available and publicized. Talking about the nuclear issue, which of these statements best describes your opinion on availability of information on this issue?

> Information on nuclear issues is easily available
> Information on nuclear issues is not so easy to get
> Information on nuclear issues is neither easy nor difficult to get
> Information on nuclear issues is difficult to get
> Information on nuclear issues is almost impossible to get

Q.5 (See Table 6)

Talking about civilian nuclear energy, the people we have met so far have expressed varying opinions about civilian nuclear energy. I will now read out some of these opinions to you. As I read out each, please tell me with the help of this card, to what extent you agree or disagree with each.

> Strongly agree
> Somewhat agree
> Neither agree nor disagree
> Somewhat disagree
> Strongly disagree
>
> **STATEMENT**
> Civilian nuclear energy program can help meet India's energy deficit
> The benefits of a civilian nuclear energy program far outweigh the costs
> A civilian nuclear energy program can be more harmful than beneficial
> The costs of a civilian nuclear energy program far outweigh its benefits

Appendix C: MARG Survey Questions

A civilian nuclear energy program has a high environmental cost attached

Q.6 (See Tables 1 and 2)

As you must be aware, India tested a nuclear device in 1974. Our official position is that we have not manufactured a nuclear weapon/device since the 1974 explosion. While India supports global disarmament on a nondiscriminatory basis, we are unwilling to close our nuclear option in the present circumstances or sign the Nonproliferation Treaty (NPT).

In light of the above, which one of these statements best describes your feelings on the issue?

STATEMENT	INSTRUCTIONS
India should maintain its official position on the nuclear issue	Go to Q.7
India should develop nuclear weapons	Go to Q.9
India should renounce nuclear weapons	Go to Q.12
No opinion/Don't know/Cannot say (only if volunteered)	Go to Q.19

Q.7 (See Table 12)
(Q.7, 8a, and 8b asked only if 1 was selected in Q.6)

You said you would like India not to renounce its nuclear option and maintain its official position on the nuclear issues.

However, in your opinion which one or more of these circumstances could justify India's developing nuclear weapons?

Pakistan tests a nuclear device
Kashmir is on the verge of secession
A serious deterioration in relations with China
A breakdown in India's relations with the Western countries
Increased turmoil in the country which requires a new rallying symbol for national unity
Threats from other nuclear powers
Threats of trade sanctions
Increased international pressures on India's domestic policies
Under no circumstances

Q.8a (See Table 7)

Could India renounce nuclear weapons under one or more of the following circumstances?

> A final boundary settlement with China and the removal of Chinese nuclear weapons from Tibet
> A verifiable renunciation of Pakistan's nuclear option
> Nuclear protection from the U.S. and/or Russia
> A threat of international sanctions
> A time-bound plan for global nuclear disarmament
> A permanent seat on the UN Security Council
> Guaranteed access to advanced technology
> Diplomatic and political support for India's position on Kashmir
> Under no circumstances

Q.8b (See Table 8)

Even if India does renounce nuclear weapons, which of these best describes your opinion on whether India should sign the NPT?

> India should sign the NPT
> –Unilaterally
> –Only if Pakistan also does the same
> –Under no circumstances

Q.9 (See Table 9)
(Q.9, 10, 11a, and 11b asked only if 2 was selected in Q. 6)

You said you want India to develop nuclear weapons. Which one or more of these are your reasons for saying this?

> Threats from China
> Threats from nuclear Pakistan
> Threats from other nuclear powers
> Threats of trade sanctions
> Increased international pressures on India's domestic policies
> To improve India's bargaining power in world affairs
> To enhance India's international status

Appendix C: MARG Survey Questions

Q.10 (See Table 13)

Even as a nuclear country, India could take various steps. Some of these are written on this card. Which one of these best describes your opinion of what India should do?

>Develop a nuclear arsenal capable of striking China and Pakistan
>Develop a nuclear arsenal capable of striking only Pakistan
>Develop a nuclear arsenal capable of striking all nuclear powers, (i.e., U.S., Russia, Pakistan, Kazakhstan, France, Britain, China, and Israel)
>Develop all the components but not actually assemble any nuclear weapon

Q.11a (See Table 7)

Could India renounce nuclear weapons under one or more of the following circumstances?

>A final boundary settlement with China and the removal of Chinese nuclear weapons from Tibet
>A verifiable renunciation of Pakistan's nuclear option
>Nuclear protection from the U.S. and/or Russia
>A threat of international sanctions
>A global ban on nuclear tests, freeze on the production of nuclear weapons material, and a time-bound plan for global nuclear disarmament
>A permanent seat on the UN Security Council
>Guaranteed access to advanced technology
>Diplomatic and political support for India's position on Kashmir
>Under no circumstances

Q.11b (See Table 8)

Even if India does renounce nuclear weapons, which of these best describes your opinion on whether India should sign the NPT?

>India should sign the NPT
> –Unilaterally
> –Only if Pakistan also does the same
> –Under no circumstances

Q.12 (See Table 10)
(Q.12, 13, and 14 asked only if 3 was selected in Q.6)

You said you would like India to renounce nuclear weapons. Which of these statements best describes the conditions on which India should renounce nuclear weapons?

>Unilaterally and sign the NPT
>Unilaterally and not sign the NPT
>Bilaterally with Pakistan and sign the NPT together
>Bilaterally with Pakistan and not sign the NPT
>Jointly with Pakistan and China

Q.13 (See Table 11)

Which one or more of these are your reasons for wanting India to renounce nuclear weapons?

>Nuclear weapons are morally repugnant
>A nuclear India would become the target of the major nuclear powers
>Nuclear weapons do not address the primary threats to India's security, i.e., terrorism and insurgency
>India cannot afford nuclear weapons
>Nuclear weapons production harms the environment

Q.14 (See Table 12)

However, would you consider India going nuclear under any of these circumstances?

>Pakistan tests a nuclear device
>Kashmir is on the verge of secession
>A serious deterioration in relations with China
>A breakdown in India's relations with the Western countries
>Increased turmoil in the country which requires a new rallying symbol for national unity
>Threats from other nuclear powers
>Threats of trade sanctions
>International pressures on India's domestic policies
>Under no circumstances

Appendix C: MARG Survey Questions

Q.15 (See Table 14)

If India does acquire a nuclear arsenal, under which of these circumstances could the nuclear weapon be used?

If Pakistan were about to take over Kashmir
If China were about to overwhelm India militarily
If a U.S.–led coalition of countries were to intervene militarily
Accidentally
Never

Q.16 (See Table 15)

To what extent do you support an international agreement for the elimination of all nuclear weapons?

Totally support
Support to an extent
Neither support nor oppose
Oppose to an extent
Totally oppose

Q.17 (See Table 16)

Do you think an international treaty banning nuclear weapons could be signed in:

The next five years?
The next ten years?
The next twenty years?
Never?

Q.18 (See Table 5)

Which of these statements is most true of you?

I have significant influence on India's nuclear policy
I have marginal influence on India's nuclear policy
I have no influence on India's nuclear policy
I am not related in any way to India's nuclear policy

Q.19 (See Table 18)

Which of these political parties, if any, do you support?

Congress (I)
Bharatiya Janata Party (BJP)
Janata Dal
CPI/CPM
SJP/BSP
Telugu Desam
AIADMK
DMK
Shiv Sena (RSS)
Muslim League
None
Others (Please specify)

Demographic Profile

Q.20 (See Table 17)

Sex of respondent

Male
Female

Q.21 (See Table 17)

Age of respondent

<39 years
40–49 years
50–59 years
60 years +

Appendix C: MARG Survey Questions

Q.22a (See Table 17)

Educational background of respondent

    Graduate (General)
    Graduate (Professional)
    Post Graduate (General)
    Post Graduate (Professional)
    Doctorate

Q.22b

Degree held:

Subject:

Q.23 (See Table 1)

Field of work

Academics	Social Work
Science	Politics
Bureaucracy	Business
Diplomacy	Armed Forces
Law	Police
Journalism	Fine Arts
Medicine	Sports
Others	

Q.24

Designation (or level) held currently/at time of retirement

Vice Chancellor	Sr. Consultant Doctor
Reader/Professor	Inspector General/(Police)
School Principal	Deputy General/(Police)
Joint Secretary	Major General or above
Above Joint Secretary	Rear Admiral or above
Member of Parliament	Air Vice Marshall or above
MLA/MLC	Chairman/MD (Private sector)
Justice-Supreme Court	Director or above (Public Sector)
Justice-High Court	Editor/Assistant Editor
Practicing Lawyer	Others (Please Specify)
Head of Hospital	Head of Department at medical university/hospital

Q.25 (See Table 17)

Have you been the recipient of any of the following awards?

National Award
Academy Award
Arjun Award
Others (Please Specify)

Bibliography

Books

Albright, David, Frans Berkhout, and William Walker. *World Inventory of Plutonium and Highly Enriched Uranium*. Oxford: SIPRI/Oxford Univ. Press, 1992.

Bailey, Kathleen C., ed. *Weapons of Mass Destruction: Costs and Benefits*. New Delhi: Manohar, 1994.

Bajpai, Kanti, P.R. Chari, Pervaiz Iqbal Cheema, Stephen P. Cohen, and Sumit Ganguly. *Brasstacks and Beyond: Perception and Management of Crisis in South Asia*. Urbana: Program in Arms Control, Disarmament and International Security, 1995.

Bhatia, Shyam. *India's Nuclear Bomb*. New Delhi: Vikas Publishing House, 1979.

Bhutto, Zulfikar A. *If I Am Assassinated*. New Delhi: Vikas Publishing House, 1979.

Blackett, P.M.S. *Fear, War, and the Bomb*. New York: Whittlesey House/McGraw Hill Book Company, 1948.

Brecher, M. *India and World Politics: K. Menon's View of the World*. London: Oxford Univ. Press, 1968.

Chari, P.R. *Indo-Pak Nuclear Standoff: The Role of the United States*. New Delhi: Manohar, 1995.

Chaudhury, J.N. *India's Problems of National Security in the Seventies*. New Delhi: United Service Institution of India, 1973.

Chellaney, Brahma. *Nuclear Proliferation: The U.S.-Indian Conflict*. New Delhi: Orient Longman, 1993.

Chopra, Pran. *India, Pakistan, and the Kashmir Tangle*. New Delhi: Indus, 1994.

Cohen, Stephen P., ed. *The Security of South Asia: Asian and American Perspectives*. Urbana, Ill. and Chicago: Univ. of Illinois Press, 1987.

———, ed. *Nuclear Proliferation in South Asia: The Prospects for Arms Control*. New Delhi: Lancers International, 1991.

Cole, Paul M. and William J. Taylor, Jr., eds. *The Nuclear Freeze Debate: Arms Control Issues for the 1980s*. Boulder, Colo.: Westview, 1991.

Committee for the Compilation of Materials on Damage Caused by the Atomic Bombs in Hiroshima and Nagasaki. *Hiroshima and Nagasaki: The Physical, Medical, and Social Effects of the Atomic Bombings*. Eisei Ishikawa and David L. Swain, trans. New York: Basic Books, 1981.

Fontana, Benedetto. *Hegemony and Power: On the Relationship Between Gramsci and Machiavelli*. Minneapolis: Univ. of Minnesota Press, 1993.

Frankel, Benjamin, ed. *Opaque Nuclear Proliferation*. London: Frank Cass, 1991.

Gaddis, John Lewis. *The Long Peace: Inquiries Into the History of the Cold War*. New York: Oxford Univ. Press, 1987.

Ganguly, Sumit. *The Origins of War in South Asia: The Indo-Pakistani Conflicts Since 1947*. Boulder, Colo.: Westview, 1994.

Gates, David. *Non-Offensive Defence: An Alternative Strategy for NATO?* London: St. Martin's, 1991.

Gerson, Joseph. *With Hiroshima Eyes: Atomic War, Nuclear Extortion, and Moral Imagination*. Philadelphia: New Society Publishers, 1995.

Hart, David. *Nuclear Power in India, A Comparative Analysis*. London: Allen and Unwin, 1983.

Hoffmann, Steven. *India and the China Crisis*. Berkeley, Calif.: The Univ. of California Press, 1990.

Jain, J.P. *Nuclear India*. New Delhi: Radiant Publishers, 1974, vol. 2.

Jasani, Bhupendra and Toshibomi Sakata, eds. *Satellites for Arms Control and Crisis Monitoring*. Oxford: SIPRI/Oxford Univ. Press, 1987.

Jones, Rodney W. *Nuclear Proliferation: Islam, the Bomb and South Asia*. The Washington Papers, vol. IX, no. 82. Beverly Hills/London: Sage Publications, 1981.

Kapur, Ashok. *India's Nuclear Option: Atomic Diplomacy and Decision Making*. New York: Praeger, 1976.

Kaushik, B.M. and O.N. Mehrotra. *Pakistan's Nuclear Bomb*. New Delhi: Sopan Publishing House, 1980.

Lal, P.C. *Some Problems of Defence*. New Delhi: United Service Institution of India, 1977.

Marwah, Onkar and Ann Schulz, eds. *Nuclear Proliferation and the Near-Nuclear Countries*. Cambridge, Mass.: Ballinger Publishing Company, 1975.

Marwah, Onkar and Jonathan D. Pollack, eds. *Military Power and Policy in Asian States: China, India, Japan*. Boulder, Colo.: Westview, 1980.

Maxwell, N. *India's China War*. Bombay: Jaico, 1971.

McNamara, Robert S. *The Changing Nature of Global Security and Its Impact on South Asia*. India International Centre, Monograph Series No. 18. New Delhi: India International Centre, 1992.

Mellor, John D., ed. *India: A Rising Middle Power*. Boulder, Colo.: Westview, 1979.

Mirchandani, G.G. *India's Nuclear Dilemma*. New Delhi: Popular Book Services, 1968.

Moeller, Bjorn. *Common Security and Non-Offensive Defense: A Neorealist Perspective*. Boulder, Colo.: Lynne Rienner, 1992.

Moshaver, Ziba. *Nuclear Weapons Proliferation in the Indian Subcontinent*. New York: St. Martin's, 1991.

Nair, Vijai K. *Nuclear India*. New Delhi: Lancers, 1992.

Nixon, Richard. *RN: The Memoirs of Richard Nixon*. New York: Grosset and Dunlap, 1978.

Nolan, Janne, ed. *Global Engagement: Cooperation and Security in the 21st Century*. Washington, D.C.: The Brookings Institution, 1994.

Nuclear Weapons and South Asian Security. Washington, D.C.: Carnegie Endowment for International Peace, 1988.

Palit, D.K. *Pakistan's Islamic Bomb*. New Delhi: Vikas Publishing House, 1979.

———. *Nuclear Shadow Over the Sub-Continent: Report of a Seminar*. New Delhi: The New Statesman Press, 1988.

Bibliography

Poulose, T.T., ed. *Perspectives of India's Nuclear Policy*. New Delhi: Young Asia Publications, 1978.

———. *Nuclear Proliferation and the Third World*. New Delhi: ABC Publishing House, 1982.

Ramberg, Bennett. *Nuclear Power Plants as Weapons for the Enemy: An Unrecognized Military Peril*. Berkeley, Calif.: Univ. of California Press, 1980.

Reiss, Mitchell. *Without the Bomb: The Politics of Nuclear Proliferation*. New York: Columbia Univ. Press, 1988.

Rizvi, Hasan Askari. *Politics of the Bomb in South Asia*. Progressive Series No. 23. Lahore, India: Progressive Publishers, 1975.

Sagan, Carl. *A Path Where No Man Thought: Nuclear Winter and the End of the Arms Race*. New York: Random House, 1990.

Schell, Jonathan. *The Abolition*. New York: Knopf, 1984.

Sen Gupta, Bhabani, ed. *Nuclear Weapons? Policy Options for India*. New Delhi: Sage Publications, 1983.

Seshagiri, N. *The Bomb: Fall-out of India's Nuclear Explosion*. New Delhi: Vikas Publishing House, 1975.

Sharma, Dhirendra. *India's Nuclear Estate*. New Delhi: Lancers, 1983.

———. *The Indian Atom: Power and Proliferation*. New Delhi: Philosophy and Social Action, 1986.

Sinha, P.B. and R.R. Subramanian. *Nuclear Pakistan: Atomic Threat to South Asia*. New Delhi: Vision Book, 1980.

Snyder, Glen. *Deterrence and Defense*. Westport. Conn.: Greenwood, 1975.

———. *Deterrence and Defense: Towards a Theory of National Security*. Princeton, N.J.: Princeton Univ. Press, 1961.

Spector, Leonard S. *Nuclear Proliferation Today*. New York: Vintage Books, 1984.

———. *The Undeclared Bomb*. Cambridge, Mass.: Ballinger Publishing Company, 1988.

Spector, Leonard S. and Jacqueline R. Smith. *Nuclear Ambitions: The Spread of Nuclear Weapons 1989–90*. Boulder, Colo.: Westview, 1990.

Spector, Leonard S. and Mark G. McDonough, with Evan S. Medeiros. *Tracking Nuclear Proliferation, A Guide in Maps and Charts, 1995*. Washington, D.C.: Carnegie Endowment for International Peace, 1995.

Sreedhar. *Pakistan's Bomb, A Documentary Study*. New Delhi: ABC Publishing House, 1986.

Subrahmanyam, K., ed. *Nuclear Myths and Realities: India's Dilemma*. New Delhi: ABC Publishing House, 1981.

———. *India's Security Perspectives*. New Delhi: ABC Publishing House, 1982.

———, ed. *Nuclear Proliferation and International Security*. New Delhi: Institute for Defence Studies and Analyses, 1985.

———, ed. *India and the Nuclear Challenge*. New Delhi: Lancers International, 1986.

Sundarji, K. *Blind Men of Hindoostan: Indo-Pak Nuclear War*. New Delhi: UBS Publishers, 1993.

Tahir-Kheli, Shirin, ed. *U.S. Strategic Interests in Southwest Asia*. New York: Praeger Publishers, 1982.

Thakur, Ramesh. *The Politics and Economics of India's Foreign Policy*. Delhi, India: Oxford Univ. Press, 1994.

Weismann, Steve and Herbert Krosney. *The Islamic Bomb*. New York: Times Books, 1981.

Williams, Shelton L. *The U.S., India and the Bomb*. Baltimore, Md.: The John Hopkins Press, 1969.

World Nuclear Industry Handbook, 1990. Sutton, Surrey, U.K.: Nuclear Engineering International, 1990.

Articles

Albright, David. "Iraq and the Bomb: Were They Even Close?" *The Bulletin of the Atomic Scientists* 47, no. 3 (March 1991).

Albright, David and Mark Hibbs. "India's Silent Bomb." *The Bulletin of the Atomic Scientists* 48, no. 7 (September 1992).

———. "Pakistan's Bomb-Making Capacity." *The Bulletin of the Atomic Scientists* 43, no. 5 (June 1987).

Albright, David and Tom Zamora. "India, Pakistan's Nuclear Weapons: All the Pieces in Place." *The Bulletin of the Atomic Scientists* 45, no. 5 (June 1989).

The Arms Control Reporter (April, 1993): 454.

Arnett, Eric. "Military Technology: The Case of India." In *SIPRI Yearbook 1994: World Armaments and Disarmament*. Oxford: Oxford Univ. Press, 1994.

Basu, Tarun and Tariq Butt. "Pakistan Says 'No' to Attempt at Dialogue." *India Abroad* 25, no. 9 (2 December 1994).

Bhargava, G.S. "India's Nuclear Policy." *India Quarterly* 34, no. 2 (April–June 1978).

Bhatia, A. "India's Space Program: Cause for Concern?" *Asian Survey* 25, no. 10 (October 1985).

Bidwai, Praful and Achin Vanaik. "India and Pakistan." In *Security With Nuclear Weapons?* edited by Regina Cowen Carp. Oxford: SIPRI/Oxford Univ. Press, 1991.

Braunthal, Gerard. "An Attitude Survey in India." *Public Opinion Quarterly* 33, no. 1 (Spring 1969).

"Bundy, Crowe, and Drell—A Program for Reducing the Nuclear Danger: But No Short Road to Disarmament." *Carnegie Quarterly* 38, nos. 3, 4 (Summer/Fall 1993).

Calogero, Francesco. "An Asymptotic Approach to a NWFW." In *A Nuclear-Weapon-Free-World: Desirable, Feasible?* edited by Joseph Rotblat, et al. Boulder, Colo.: Westview, 1993.

Chari, P.R. "An Indian Reaction to U.S. Non-Proliferation Policy." *International Security* 3, no. 2 (Fall 1978).

———. "How to Prevent a Nuclear Arms Race Between India and Pakistan." In *Regional Cooperation in South Asia*, vol. 1, edited by Bhabani Sen Gupta. New Delhi: South Asia Publishers, 1986.

Chawla, J. "A Nuclear India." *Seminar* no. 146 (October 1971).

Cheema, Zafar Iqbal. "Nuclear Diplomacy in South Asia During the 1980s." *Regional Studies* 1, no. 3 (Summer 1992).

Chellaney, Brahma. "An Indian Critique of U.S. Export Controls." *Orbis* 38, no. 3 (Summer 1994).

Chopra, Pran. "For a World Freed of the Nuclear Menace." In *The Diffusion of Advanced Weaponry: Technologies, Regional Implications, and Responses*, edited by W. Thomas Wander, Eric H. Arnett, and Paul Bracken. Washington, D.C.: American Association for the Advancement of Science, 1994.

Collina, Tom Zamora. "Cutoff Talks Delayed." *The Bulletin of the Atomic Scientists* 51, no. 2 (March/April 1995).

Dunn, Lewis A. "Half Past India's Bang." *Foreign Policy* no. 36 (Fall 1979).

———. "Rethinking the Nuclear Equation: The United States and the New Nuclear Powers." *The Washington Quarterly* 17, no. 5 (Winter 1994).

Ellsberg, Daniel. "Introduction: A Call to Mutiny." In *Protest and Survive*, edited by E.P. Thompson and Dan Smith. New York: Monthly Review Press, 1981.

Gandhi, M.K. "Atom Bomb and Ahimsa." *Harijan* (Poona), 7 July 1946.

———. "With an English Journalist." *Harijan* (New Delhi), 29 September 1946.

Ganguly, Sumit. "Nuclear Issues in South Asia." In *The Diffusion of Advanced Weaponry: Technologies, Regional Implications, and Responses*, edited by W. Thomas Wander, Eric H. Arnett, and Paul Bracken. Washington, D.C.: American Association for the Advancement of Science, 1994.

Garwin, Richard. "Nuclear Weapons for the United Nations." In *A Nuclear-Weapon-Free-World: Desirable, Feasible?*, edited by Joseph Rotblat, et al. Boulder, Colo.: Westview, 1993.

Gordon, Sandy. "Capping South Asia's Nuclear Weapons Programs: A Window of Opportunity?" *Asian Survey* 34, no. 7 (July 1994).

Gupta, Sisir K. "The Indian Dilemma." In *A World of Nuclear Powers*, edited by Alastair Buchan. Englewood Cliffs, N.J.: Prentice Hall, 1966.

Haas, Peter. "Introduction: Epistemic Communities and International Policy Coordination." *International Organization* 46, no. 1 (Winter 1992).

Haass, Richard. "South Asia: Too Late to Remove the Bomb." *Orbis* 32, no. 1 (Winter 1988).

Hagerty, Devin T. "The Power of Suggestion: Opaque Proliferation, Existential Deterrence, and the South Asian Nuclear Competition." *Security Studies* 2, nos. 3/4 (Spring/Summer 1993).

Hersh, Seymour. "On The Nuclear Edge." *The New Yorker*, 29 March 1993.

Holmes, Steven A. "China Denies Violating Pact By Selling Arms to Pakistan." *The New York Times*, 26 July 1993.

IDR Research Team. "Grappling With the Dynamics of Nuclear Strategy: Policy Formulation for a Nuclear India." *Indian Defence Review*, July 1989.

———. "Nuclear China: The Equation with India." *Indian Defence Review*, July 1989.

Iqbal, Mohammed. "India's Space Programme." *Regional Studies* (Islamabad) 2, no. 1 (Winter 1983).

Jain, Girilal. "India." Chap. 5A in *Non Proliferation: The Why and the Wherefore*, edited by Jozef Goldblat. London: SIPRI/Taylor and Francis, 1985.

Jones, Rodney. "India." Chap. 5B in *Non Proliferation: The Why and the Wherefore*, edited by Jozef Goldblat. London: SIPRI/Taylor and Francis, 1985.

Kapur, Ashok. "India and the Atom." *The Bulletin of the Atomic Scientists* 30, no. 7 (September 1974).

———. "Western Biases." *The Bulletin of the Atomic Scientists* 51, no. 1 (January/February 1995).

Krishna, Raj. "India and the Bomb." *India Quarterly* 21, no. 2 (April–June 1965).

Leonard, James F. and Adam M. Scheinman. "Denuclearizing South Asia: Global Approaches to a Regional Problem." *Arms Control Today* 23, no. 5 (June 1993).

Marwah, Onkar. "India's Nuclear and Space Programs: Intent and Policy." *International Security* 2, no. 2 (Fall 1977).

Matilal, Bimal Krishna. "Between Peace and Deterrence." In *Peace Studies: The Hard Questions*, edited by Elaine Kaye, Oxford Peace Lectures 1984–85. London: Rex Collings, 1987.

Mattoo, Amitabh. "Sanctions, Incentives and Nuclear Proliferation: The Case of India." *Journal of Peace Studies* (July/August 1994).

Milhollin, Gary. "Dateline New Delhi: India's Nuclear Cover-up." *Foreign Policy* no. 64 (Fall 1986).

———. "India's Missiles: With a Little Help from Our Friends." *The Bulletin of the Atomic Scientists* 45, no. 9 (November 1989).

Mohan, C. Raja. "India's Nuclear Policy at the Crossroads." In *The Director's Series on Proliferation*, edited by Kathleen C. Bailey. California: Lawrence Livermore National Laboratory, 1993.

Muang, Mya. "On the Road to Mandalay: A Case Study of the Sinoization of Upper Burma." *Asian Survey* 34, no. 5 (May 1994).

Munro, Ross H. "The Asian Interior: China's Waxing Spheres of Influence." *Orbis* 38, no. 4 (Fall 1994).

Naim, Rashid. "After Midnight." In *Nuclear Proliferation in South Asia*, edited by Stephen P. Cohen. Boulder, Colo.: Westview, 1991.

Nandy, Ashis. "Between Two Gandhis: Psychopolitical Aspects of the Nuclearization of India." *Asian Survey* 14, no. 11 (1974).

———. "The Bomb, the NPT, and Indian Elites." *Economic and Political Weekly* (Bombay), Special Number, (August 1982).

Naqvi, M.B. "The Nuclear Mirage." *Newsline*, April 1994.

Narain, Jayaprakash. "India, China and Peace." *Anarchy* 4, no. 8 (August 1964).

———. "India and the Bomb: A Symposium." *Gandhi Marg* 10, no. 1 (January 1966).

Neuhoff, Jon and Clifford Singer. "Verification and Control of Fissile Materials." In *Nuclear Proliferation in South Asia: The Prospects for Arms Control*, edited by Stephen P. Cohen. Boulder, Colo.: Westview, 1991.

Noorani, A.G. "India's Quest for a Nuclear Guarantee." *Asian Survey* 7, no. 7 (July 1967).

———. "India-U.S. Nuclear Relations." *Asian Survey* 21, no. 4 (April 1981).

Ollapally, Deepa and Raja Ramanna. "US-India Tensions." *Foreign Affairs* 74, no. 1 (January/February 1995).

Perkovich, George. "A Nuclear Third Way in South Asia." *Foreign Policy* no. 91 (Summer 1993).

———. "Three Models for Nuclear Policy in South Asia: The Case for Non-Weaponised Deterrence." In *The Road Ahead: Indo-US Strategic Dialogue*, edited by Jasjit Singh. New Delhi: Lancers International, 1994.

Bibliography

Quester, George H. "Can Proliferation Now Be Stopped?" *Foreign Affairs* 53, no. 1 (October 1974).

———. "India Contemplates the Bomb." *The Bulletin of the Atomic Scientists* 26, no. 1 (January 1970).

Ramanna, Raja. "Limits and Limitations." In *National Security and Modern Technology*, by Raja Ramanna. New Delhi: United Service Institution of India, 1988.

Rao, R.V.R. Chandrashekhara. "India and the Nuclear Weapons Option: Eclipse of the Ethical Profile." *Swords and Ploughshares*, May 1987.

Reiss, Mitchell. "The United States and Pakistan's Nuclear Programme." *The RUSI Journal*, (Summer 1991).

———. "Safeguarding the Nuclear Peace in South Asia." *Asian Survey* 33, no. 12 (December 1993).

Schulz, John J. "Riding the Nuclear Tiger: The Search for Security in South Asia." *Arms Control Today* 23, no. 5 (June 1993).

Shambaugh, David. "Growing Strong: China's Challenge to Asian Security." *Survival* 36, no. 2 (Summer 1994).

Shen, Dingli. "The Prospects for a Comprehensive Test Ban Treaty: Implications of Chinese Nuclear Testing." In *Diffusion of Advanced Weaponry: Technologies, Regional Implications, and Responses* edited by W. Thomas Wander, Eric H. Arnett, and Paul Bracken. Washington, D.C.: American Association for the Advancement of Science, 1994.

Singh, Jasjit. "Prospects for Nuclear Proliferation." In *Nuclear Deterrence: Problems and Perspectives in the 1990's*, edited by Serge Sur. New York: United Nations, 1993.

Subrahmanyam, K. "Implications of Nuclear Asymmetry." In *Nuclear Myths and Realities: India's Dilemma* edited by K. Subrahmanyam. New Delhi: ABC Publishing, 1981.

———. "Nuclear Force Design and Minimum Deterrence Strategy for India." In *Future Imperilled: India's Security in the 1990s and Beyond* edited by Bharat Karnad. New Delhi: Viking, 1994.

Subramaniam, R.R. and K. Subrahmanyam. "Mutual Inspection and Verification." In *India and the Nuclear Challenge* edited by K. Subrahmanyam. New Delhi: Lancers, 1986.

Sun, Lena H. "China, India Sign Accord To Ease Border Dispute." *The Washington Post*, 8 September 1993.

Sundarji, K. "Indian Nuclear Doctrine-II: Sino-Indo-Pak Triangle." *Indian Express*, 26 November 1994.

Tahir-Kheli, Shirin. "Pakistan's Nuclear Option and US Policy." *Orbis* 22, no. 2 (Summer 1978).

Thomas, Raju. "India." In *Energy and Security in the Industrializing World* edited by Raju G.C. Thomas and Bennett Ramberg. Lexington, Ky.: The University Press of Kentucky, 1990.

Vanaik, Achin. "Political Case for a NWFZ in South Asia." *Economic and Political Weekly* 10, no. 48 (30 November 1985).

Government Documents, Dissertations, Occasional Papers

Bajpai, Kanti and Varun Sahni. *Secure and Solvent: Thinking About an Affordable Defence for India*, RGICS Paper No. 11, Rajiv Gandhi Institute for Contemporary Studies, New Delhi, May 1994.

Barker, Robert. "Costs of US Nuclear Weapons Program." Paper prepared for the conference on "Proliferation: A Cost/Benefit Analysis." New Delhi, 8–9 November 1993.

Bouton, Marshall, et al. *Preventing Proliferation in South Asia: The Report of a Study Group*. The Asia Society, New York, N.Y., 1994.

The Carnegie Study Group on U.S.-Indian Relations in a Changing International Environment. Washington, D.C.: Carnegie Endowment for International Peace, 1992.

"Documents: Resolutions Adopted at the NPT Extension Conference." *Arms Control Today* 25, no. 5 (June 1995).

"Effects of Nuclear Asymmetry on Conventional Deterrence." Combat Paper No. 1, College of Combat, Mhow, India, May 1981.

El Assal, Elaine. "Indian Elites Support Three-Way Regional Nuclear Freeze But Reject Unilateral Cap." M-128-94, United States Information Agency *Opinion Research Memorandum*, 27 May 1994.

———. "Most Urban Indians Still Oppose NPT." M-20-95, United States Information Agency *Opinion Analysis*, 27 January 1995.

Gandhi, Rajiv. *A World Free of Nuclear Weapons: An Action Plan*. Address to Third Special Session on Disarmament, UN General Assembly, 9 June 1988. Printed by Rajiv Gandhi Foundation, New Delhi.

Ganguly, Sumit. *Slouching Towards a Settlement: Sino-Indian Relations, 1962–1993*. Asia Program Monograph No. 60, The Woodrow Wilson International Center for Scholars, Washington D.C. 1990.

Government of India. *Disarmament: India's Initiatives*. External Publicity Division, New Delhi, Ministry of External Affairs, 1988.

Joeck, Neil. *Nuclear Weapons Issues in South Asia*. Center for Security and Technology Studies, Lawrence Livermore National Laboratory, CSTS-43-93 dated 2 July 1993.

Krepon, Michael and Mishi Faruqee, eds. *Conflict Prevention and Confidence-Building Measures in South Asia: The 1990 Crisis*. Washington, D.C.: The Henry L. Stimson Center, April 1994.

Mattoo, Amitabh. "The Campaign for Nuclear Disarmament: A Study of its Reemergence, Growth and Decline in the 1980s." D. Phil. diss., Faculty of Social Studies, University of Oxford, 1992.

Namboodiri, P.K.S. "China-Pakistan Nuclear Axis." *Strategic Analysis*, New Delhi: IDSA, October 1982.

Nehru, Jawaharlal. *India's Foreign Policy, Select Speeches, September 1946 to April 1961*, Publications Division, Ministry of Information and Broadcasting, Government of India, New Delhi, 1961.

Noorani, A.G. *Easing the Indo-Pakistan Dialogue on Kashmir*. Washington, D.C.: The Henry L. Stimson Center, Occasional Paper No. 17, April 1994.

Sandrock, John and Michael Maldony. *The History and Future of Confidence Building Measures in South Asia: A Background Paper*. McLean, Va.: Science Applications International Corporation (SAIC), 1994.

Bibliography

Study on the Climatic and Other Global Effects of Nuclear War. A/43/351, Department for Disarmament Affairs, Report to the Secretary General, New York: United Nations, 1989.

Stumpf, Waldo. "South Africa's Nuclear Weapons Programme." Paper prepared for the conference on "Proliferation: A Cost/Benefit Analysis." New Delhi, 8–9 November 1993.

Subrahmanyam, K. "Nuclear Policy, Arms Control and Military Cooperation." Paper presented at a conference on "India and the United States After the Cold War," sponsored by the India International Center and Carnegie Endowment for International Peace, New Delhi, 7–9 March 1993.

Wohlstetter, R. "The Buddha Smiles: Absent-Minded Peaceful Aid and the Indian Bomb." Energy Research and Development Administration (Monograph 3, 30 April 1977).

Index

A

Action Plan, Non-Violent World Order 8, 63, 64
Advani, Lal Kishan 10, 89
Afghan War 73
Agni 8, 70, 72, 78, 93, 94
All horizons nuclear capability 95, 96, 97, 101
All India Radio 59
Antinuclear movement 48
Antinuclear organizations 6
Argentina 28
Asia 35, 70
Asia Society 75
Atomic Energy Act of 1962 6
Atoms for Peace plan 56
Australia 103

B

Bahadur, Lal Shastri 7
Bajpai, Kanti 4, 23
Ballistic missile submarines (SSBNs) 94, 95, 97, 100, 103
Ballistic missile technology 65
Ballistic missiles 76. *See also* Submarine-launched ballistic missiles
Bangalore 11
Bangladesh 86
Banihal Tunnel 37
Baruch Plan 28
Bay of Bengal 70
Beijing 9, 12, 18, 35, 58, 77
Bhabha, Homi J. 54, 57, 59, 90
Bharatiya Janata Party (BJP) 9, 10, 13, 47, 89, 98

Bhutto, Benazir 71, 86
Bhutto, Zulfikar 86
Bihar 61
Bilateral arms control 18
Bilateral nuclear agreement 12
Bilateral test ban 64
Bombay 11, 12, 55, 59
Brahmastra 89
Brasstacks 70
Brazil 28
Britain 54, 94, 96, 100, 102
British Commonwealth Foreign Secretaries 71
British/French Jaguar 8
Burma 70
Burmese coast 70

C

Calcutta 11, 12, 59
Calogero, Francesco 28
Canada 58, 61, 72
Central Asian republics 64
Central European theater 103
Chaudhury, J.N. 89
China 7, 9, 10, 12, 14, 15, 16, 18, 24, 26, 28, 29, 31, 32, 35, 36, 38, 42, 54, 57, 58, 63, 64, 69, 70, 71, 73, 74, 75, 77, 78, 80, 86, 87, 92, 93, 94, 95, 98, 102, 103, 104
Chinese first strike 93
Chinese missiles 87
Chinese nuclear arsenals 64
Chinese territorial gains 70
Chopra, Pran 28
City University/Hunter College 5
Civilian nuclear energy program 13

155

Cold war 27, 64, 87
Command and control (C³I) 76, 92, 94, 96, 98
Committee for a Sane Nuclear Policy 6
Communists 59, 98
Comprehensive test ban (CTB) 29, 33, 34, 69, 76, 75, 77, 79, 80. *See also* Bilateral test ban
Comprehensive Test Ban Treaty (CTBT) 5, 7, 9, 18, 75, 76, 77, 80
Computer-simulated testing 34
Confidence-building measures 70
Congress party 13, 59, 98
Conventional Forces in Europe (CFE) 39
Crisis in 1990 3
Cuban Missile Crisis 3, 43
Currency of power 88

D

Delhi 6
Desai, Morarji 61, 62
Deuterium 72
Dhruva 72
Disarmament 5, 18. *See also* Phased global disarmament
Dixit, Aabha 4, 53
Dutch 62

E

East/West confrontation 27, 101
Economic sanctions 42
Eisenhower, Dwight D. 56
English press 47
Europe 27

F

F-16 73
Fast Breeder Test Reactor 8
First strike 102
Fissile material 33, 91, 92, 100
 ban on production of 5, 7, 8, 9, 18, 63, 69, 75, 76, 77, 79, 80
 cutoff regime 78, 79
 stockpiles 78
Force de frappe 95, 96

France 28, 29, 31, 32, 63, 87, 94, 95, 100, 102

G

Gandhi, Indira 7, 59, 60, 61, 62
Gandhi, Mohandas K. 5, 6, 16, 48, 54, 56, 66
Gandhi, Rajiv 8, 29, 63
Gandhian 25, 26, 48, 54, 57, 61, 62
Ganguly, Sumit 5, 69
Garwin, Richard 28
GATT 13
Geneva 59
Geosynchronous Satellite Launch Vehicle 95
Germany 36, 44, 64, 94, 102
Global nonproliferation regime 65
Gordon, Sandy 75
Gujarat 61
Gulf War 56

H

Harijan 54
Hatf I and *Hatf II* missiles 73
Hersh, Seymour 3
Himalayan border 70
Himalayas 36, 87
Hindu 11, 89
Hiroshima 6, 38
Horizontal proliferation 63
House of Tatas 54
Hyderabad 11

I

India
 Atomic Energy Act 55
 Atomic Energy Commission (AEC) 5, 7, 54, 90
 civilian nuclear energy program 8
 Defence Research and Development Organisation (DRD) 72, 96
 Defence Science Organisation 55
 Department of Space 96
 disarmament initiatives 64
 domestic politics 45
 foreign policy 57

intellectual community 47
Ministry of Defence 46
Ministry of External Affairs 46
National Security Council (NSC) 46
nuclear policy 4, 8, 10, 12, 14, 45, 47, 48, 53, 54, 56, 57, 59, 61, 62, 63, 65, 66
Parliament 5, 7, 11, 55, 60, 65
India disarmament initiatives 54, 55
   Cessation of All Explosions 56
   Composition of the Disarmament Commission 56
   Declaration on Removal of Threat of New War 55
   Directives on General and Complete Disarmament 56
   Dissemination of Information, Effects of Radiation 55
   Peaceful Uses of Atomic Energy 55
   Suspension of Nuclear and Thermonuclear Tests 56
Indian Defence Research/Development Organisation 8
Indian National Science Academy 90
Indian Ocean 64, 88, 97, 103
Indian press 47
Indian Space Research Organisation (ISRO) 95
Indo-Gangetic Plain 95
Indo-Soviet Treaty of Peace, Friendship 87
Indonesia 103
Institute of Defence Studies and Analyses (IDSA) 4, 90
Integrated Missile Development Programme (IMDP) 95, 96
Intercontinental ballistic missile (ICBM) 91, 93, 94, 95, 96
Intermediate Nuclear Forces treaty (INF) 39
Intermediate-range ballistic missiles (IRBMs) 93, 94
International Atomic Energy Agency (IAEA) 8, 28, 33, 56, 57, 64, 69, 71, 72, 73
   IAEA Statute, Article II 56
Iraq 33, 34, 96, 97
Ireland 59

Islamabad 9, 16, 18, 39, 41, 45, 62, 64, 71, 73, 75
Islamic 64
Islamic bomb 86
Israel 28, 65

J

Jan Sangh 59
Japan 36, 38, 63, 101, 102
Jawaharlal Nehru University 4, 5
Jones, Rodney 57, 65
Joshi, Murli Manohar 89

K

Kahuta 73
Kakrapar 71
Karachi 72
Kashmir 3, 13, 14, 15, 36, 37, 38, 42, 43, 44, 70, 71, 74, 87
Kazakhstan 28
Kerala 72
Kerr, Richard J. 3
Khan, Abdul Qadir 62
Korea 28, 35
Kroc Institute 10, 23, 24, 25, 29, 30, 32, 36, 41, 46, 53, 62, 65, 70, 71, 79, 80, 86, 87, 88, 89, 91, 96, 97, 98, 104

L

Lakshmana Rekha 85
Leonard, James 75
London Nuclear Supplier's Club 72
Lop Nor 58
Lucknow 11, 12

M

M-11 missile 73, 78, 79
Madras 11, 12, 59
Mahabharata 89
Marketing and Research Group Pvt. Ltd. (MARG) 10
Mattoo, Amitabh 3, 97
Menon, Krishna 55
MiG 92
MiG-23 8

MiG-27 8, 72
Minh, Ho Chi 38
Minimal nuclear capability 92, 101, 103
Mirage 93
Moral opposition 54
Moscow 56
Mukherjee, Pranab 9

N

Nagasaki 6, 38
Naim, Rashid 101, 102
Nair, Vijai K. 94, 99, 100
National Security Lecture 89
Nehru, Jawaharlal 5, 7, 17, 49, 53, 54, 55, 57, 59, 66, 90, 102
Nehruvian model 58, 62
Neuhoff, Jon 77
New Delhi 3, 4, 5, 6, 7, 9, 10, 11, 12, 16, 17, 18, 29, 30, 31, 33, 36, 37, 46, 53, 56, 59, 60, 62, 63, 64, 65, 70, 74, 79, 102
Nixon, Richard 38
No first use 87, 103
No-bomb lobby 58, 60
Non-weaponized deterrence 74
Nongovernmental organizations (NGOs) 48
Nonnuclear option 102
Nonweaponized nuclear capability 92, 101
Nonweaponized nuclear posture 91, 103
North Atlantic Treaty Organization (NATO) 103
North Korea 28, 32, 33, 34
Nuclear
  abstinence 23, 24, 25, 41, 43, 46, 48, 49
  ambiguity 42, 44
  arms race 102, 103
  asymmetry 35, 36, 37, 86, 88, 99
  attack 27, 37, 38, 40
  capability 4, 8, 12, 53, 59, 71, 75, 87, 88, 89, 90, 95, 96, 98, 99, 101
  confrontation 3
  debate 3, 5, 6
  decision making 5
  deterrence 9, 41, 42, 43, 44, 45
  disarmament 6, 7, 8, 12, 14, 16, 18, 24, 26, 30, 53, 55, 57, 63, 66, 79, 102, 104
  exchange 3
  freeze 5, 69, 71, 73, 74, 75, 77, 78, 79, 80
  guarantees 41
  option 4, 6, 11, 12, 14, 17, 18, 24, 30, 39, 58, 59, 65, 85, 86, 90, 91, 92, 93, 94, 95, 96
  policy 4, 5, 6, 13, 85
  powers 25, 26, 28, 29, 39, 42, 102, 104
  test ban 63
  testing 71, 101
  threat 24, 25, 26, 37, 38, 39, 40, 42, 50
  umbrella 25, 27, 29, 30, 37, 87
  verification 74
Nuclear Nonproliferation Treaty (NPT) 7, 9, 10, 16, 18, 25, 26, 30, 31, 32, 33, 34, 41, 48, 53, 54, 58, 59, 60, 61, 63, 65, 66, 75, 88, 96, 104
  violations 34
Nuclear Nonproliferation Treaty Extension/Review C 9, 16, 29, 32, 48, 64, 65
Nuclear test at Pokhran, 1974 61, 102
Nuclear weapon-free zone 64
Nuclear weapons state (NWS) 33, 64, 88, 96, 98, 101

O

Official Secrets Act 6, 90

P

Pakistan 3, 9, 10, 11, 12, 14, 15, 16, 17, 18, 24, 26, 27, 28, 29, 30, 32, 33, 34, 36, 39, 40, 42, 43, 45, 53, 62, 63, 64, 66, 69, 70, 72, 73, 74, 75, 76, 77, 78, 80, 86, 87, 88, 89, 93, 94, 95, 97, 102, 103
Paris 54
Parliament 32
Parliamentary Committee for Foreign Affairs 9

Partial Test Ban Treaty (PTBT) 56
Perkovich, George 74, 75, 91
Phased global disarmament 27, 29, 30, 41
Plutonium 72, 73, 77
Pokhran 61, 62, 102, 103
Polar Satellite Launch Vehicle 95
Pressler Amendment to the Foreign Assistance Act 73
Prithvi 8, 70, 72, 78, 79, 93, 94
Pro-bomb 87, 88, 89
Pro-bomb lobby 9, 10, 57, 58, 59, 60, 62
Program of Action on Disarmament 7
Punjab 37, 87

R

Radioactive contamination 101
Rajasthan 61
Ramanna, Raja 90
Ramayana 89
Rao, P.V. Narasimha 62, 63, 64
Reagan, Ronald 73
Reiss, Mitchell 73
Russia 28, 29, 31, 33, 34, 36, 38, 39, 42, 44, 56, 63, 64, 87, 93, 95, 96, 100, 101, 102

S

Sahni, Varun 5, 85
Sanctions 15, 42, 97, 102
Scheinman, Adam M. 75
Second World War 44, 88, 94
Security threats 99
Sharif, Nawaz 86
Shastri, Lal Bahadur 59
Short-range ballistic missiles (SRBMs) 93, 94, 96
Sindh 37
Singer, Clifford 77
Sino-Indian border agreement 70
Snyder, Glenn 74
Socialists 59
South Africa 32, 85, 103
South Asia 9, 12, 16, 18, 39, 43, 44, 62, 63, 64, 69, 71, 73, 74, 75, 76, 80, 85, 92, 101, 104

Srinivasan, Krishnan 71
Stability/instability paradox 74
Standstill Agreement 7, 55
Strategic ambiguity 4, 53
Submarine-launched ballistic missiles (SLBMs) 94
Subrahmanyam, K. 9, 88, 90, 92, 93, 99, 100
Sundarji, K. 87, 92
Survey results
   Availability of Information 13
   Biographic Characteristics 13
   Extent of Developing Nuclear Weapons 15
   Justifying Development of Nuclear Weapons 12, 14
   Nuclear Opponents: Reasons for Renunciation 16
   Opinion on the Civilian Nuclear Energy Program 13
   Political Affiliation 13
   Possible Use Of Nuclear Weapons 15
   Potential Impact of Sanctions 15
   Regions 12
   Renouncing Nuclear Weapons 14
   Salience 13
   Views on Arms Control Issues 16
Swatantra Party 59

T

Tata Institute for Fundamental Research 54
Thorium 72
Tibet 14, 18, 35, 42, 70, 74, 87
Tous azimuths 15, 95, 96
Transparency 80, 91, 99, 100
Triad nuclear capability 93, 101, 103
Tritium 72
Trombay 72

U

Ukraine 28
United Kingdom 28, 29, 31, 63

United Nations 7, 28, 29, 31, 55, 57, 58, 75, 76
   Article 43, UN Charter 28
   Conference on Disarmament 76
   Disarmament Commission 55, 56
   Eighteen Nation Disarmament Commission 58, 59
   General Assembly 54, 55, 61, 63, 76
   Military Staff Committee 28
   Second Special Session on Disarmament 7
   Security Council 14, 31, 63, 64, 88
   Special Session on Disarmament 63
United Service Institution of India 89
United States 8, 10, 16, 18, 26, 27, 28, 29, 31, 32, 34, 38, 42, 44, 56, 58, 61, 63, 64, 73, 75, 78, 87, 88, 93, 95, 96, 97, 101, 102
   Central Intelligence Agency 3
   Congress 73
   Nuclear Non-Proliferation Act (NNPA) 72
   Soviet competition 103
U.S. Information Agency 31, 32, 79, 80
Uranium 235 72, 73, 77
URENCO 62
Uttar Pradesh 11

V

Verification 5, 91
Vietnam 35, 38

W

Warsaw Pact 103
Weapons-grade plutonium 66
Western countries 14, 24, 61, 65, 66, 86, 101
Western Europe 26
Western Hemisphere 91

X

Xinkiang 35, 87

Y

Yugoslavia 28

Z

Zero-yield tests 34